History  & Guide

COLCHESTER

History & Guide

COLCHESTER

Patrick Denney

TEMPUS

For Anna

Frontispiece: *Imaginative reconstruction of Norman Colchester by Peter Frost.*

First published 2004

Tempus Publishing Ltd
The Mill, Brimscombe Port
Stroud, Gloucestershire GL5 2QG

British Library Cataloguing in Publication Data.
A catalogue record for this book is available from the British Library.

ISBN 0 7524 3214 1

Typesetting and origination by Tempus Publishing.
Printed in Great Britain by Midway Colour Print, Wiltshire

Contents

Preface & Acknowledgements

I am pleased to present this new history of Colchester, including a walking tour, as an addition to the existing range of publications already dealing with various aspects of the subject. My intention from the beginning has been to provide a concise yet comprehensive history of the town, covering all the main historical periods and highlights. Due to restrictions on space, however, much has had to be omitted, but hopefully what has been included will prove to be an acceptable narrative and serve to whet the reader's appetite for delving even deeper into the town's rich and fascinating history.

The walking tour section follows closely to the route taken by the town's Blue Badge guides, with whom I am pleased to be associated. To follow the tour in its entirety would probably take about two hours to complete, but the design is such that allows for as many stops and starts as may be necessary, aided by an easy-to-follow map.

At the end of the book is a brief section providing information on recommended further reading for those wishing to enhance their study of a particular subject area.

I am greatly indebted to a number of people who have provided valuable information and assistance in support of the publication of this book. In particular I would like to make special mention of the help given by the following groups and individuals: Peter Frost and the Colchester Archaeological Trust for permission to reproduce a number of reconstruction drawings of Roman and Norman Colchester, and other archaeological material; the Museum Resource Centre for permission to make use of copyright material in their possession and Brian Light for his assistance in producing the street plan for the walking tour. In addition, I would like to thank the following individuals who have each provided me with valued help and assistance: Derek Blowers, Philip Crummy, Charles Debenham, Christine Denney, Stephen Denney, Joan Dobson, Peter Evans, Frank Gardiner, John Gardner, Peter Haines, John Hedges, Andrea Hitchcock and David Snow. If I have made any omissions, it is with regret and in no way intentional.

Patrick Denney
Colchester, February 2004

CHAPTER 1

Celts and Romans

It is difficult to determine precisely when Colchester's long history began. We know from archaeological evidence that there must have been a presence here during the Neolithic and Bronze Age periods, but it is really only from the late Iron Age that Colchester, or Camulodunum (which means 'fortress of Camulos' – the war god) as it was then known, enters into the age of recorded history.

The Celtic people who inhabited this area were the Trinovantes, one of twenty or so tribes scattered throughout Britain, each with their own king or queen. The Trinovantian kingdom covered an area roughly equal to present-day Essex and south Suffolk, and by the early first century AD had become the dominant power in the country. This was due largely to their ruler Cunobelin, a powerful king who has also passed into history as Shakespeare's Cymbeline. The Roman historian, Suetonius, styled him *Britanniorum rex* (king of the Britons), and it was into his former kingdom that the invading Roman army marched in AD 43.

Cunobelin was, in fact, a member of the powerful Catuvellaunian tribe who inhabited land to the west of the Trinovantes, in modern Hertfordshire. When Julius Caesar's army invaded Britain in 54 BC, it was the Catuvellauni, under the leadership of Cassivellaunus, one of Cunobelin's ancestors, who provided the stiffest resistance to the Roman advance. One of the reasons why Caesar had invaded Britain at this time was in response to a request for help from Mandubracius, a member of the Trinovantes, whose father had apparently been killed by Cassivellaunus. Caesar's army finally overcame the British resistance and Cassivellaunus, among others, was forced to pay an annual tribute to Rome, and to maintain peaceful relations with Mandubracius and the Trinovantes.

The years following Caesar's invasion are sketchy and it is not until coins are discovered from around 20 BC that we find further clues as to what was happening. For example, we know that from about 15 BC the Catuvellaunian kingdom was ruled by Tasciovanus, who was one of the first rulers to put his name and mint mark on his coins. At first the place named on the coins issued by Tasciovanus is Verulamium (St Albans), but from about 10 BC we also find coins of Tasciovanus with the Camulodunum (Colchester) mint mark. This would seem to imply that a conquest of the Trinovantes had taken place and that Tasciovanus had set up his tribal capital at Camulodunum. Whether Camulodunum was in fact a new Catuvellaunian outpost in Trinovantian territory, or perhaps an existing Trinovantian settlement, is not clear, and over the next few years other kings from both camps continued to produce coins with the Camulodunum mint mark.

Finally, from around AD 5 we begin to find a long run of coins issued by Cunobelin (the son of Tasciovanus) at Camulodunum. The Catuvellauni had clearly extended their territory into Essex, which provided them with direct access to the sea, and it would appear that both tribes had by now become united under one royal household. We referred earlier to the fact that the Romans knew all about Cunobelin and his capital at Camulodunum, but what kind of set-tlement would it have been? Clearly is was nothing like a modern town or city, but perhaps something more akin to a large farming complex with industrial and commercial outlets.

We know that the site itself was quite large and may well have extended over an area equivalent to much of the modern town stretching from Donyland and Berechurche in the east to Lexden and Stanway in the west, although the two principal areas excavated so far have been centred on Gosbecks and Sheepen. The Gosbecks area is located a little to the west of the modern town, and appears to have been the residential centre of the community, and perhaps where the royal household itself was located. The Sheepen site occu-pied lower ground close to the River Colne, and was where various kinds of manufacturing and trading took place. The whole area, however, was heavily defended by a series of banks and ditches which enclosed an area of some 12 square miles (30 km²). Over the years, the Gosbecks site has revealed a vast amount of information about how the site may have been viewed and operated. Of particu-lar note are the foundation ditches of a large Roman theatre, which would have seated in excess of 5,000, and a Roman temple with colonnaded portico. Other features discovered include a whole range of enclosures, ditches, trackways and the remains of at least one wooden water-pipe system.

Adjacent to Gosbecks is Stanway, where a number of Romano-British burial sites have been discovered, dating from the late first century BC to around AD 60. The graves are contained within sev-eral large enclosures, some of which appear to be those of high-status individuals, judging by some of the grave goods recovered. One of the most exciting discoveries, however, has come from one of the smaller secondary graves in the corner of one of the enclosures. This is the so-called 'doctor's grave', where the remains of a Roman gaming board, complete with the opposing counters set out ready to play, was found. Also discovered in the grave was a complete set of surgical instruments, most of which can be easily identified by modern doctors.

The Sheepen site was extensively excavated in the 1930s, when a whole array of finds of an industrial nature were recorded. These included numerous coins and fragments of coin moulds, pieces of glass and bone and literally tons of broken pottery. Moreover, evidence of metalworking was easy to detect through the remains of hearths, ovens and waste products associated with the activity.

It is also extremely likely that some kind of harbour or landing stage would have been located fairly close to the Sheepen site, and that small sailing vessels would have made their way up river a mile or so beyond the present harbour area, through what is now Castle Park. Fortunately, we also have a fair idea as to what these sailing vessels might have looked like, thanks to the chance discovery of two rare Iron Age coins. The two coins, one found at Canterbury in 1978 and the other in the River Colne in 1980, were both minted at Camulodunum and depict an Iron Age sailing vessel. The ships depicted are tall, with deep sides, and not at all like the shallower-hulled Roman models. These are, in fact, the only images of an Iron Age sailing vessel known to exist, and are thus of particular interest to maritime historians.

The 'doctor's grave' at Stanway, showing excavation work on the Roman board game.

Drawing of an Iron Age sailing vessel on the River Colne, by Frank Gardiner.

Cunobelin's rule lasted for about forty years until his death in *c.* AD 40. He had become the most powerful of the British kings, and the leader of a confederacy of Celtic tribes extending throughout much of south-east England. He was also the last of the ancient British sovereigns to die a powerful and free man.

Following his death it might have been expected that his kingdom would have been divided between his three sons, Adminius, Togodumnus and Caractacas. This indeed was partly the case, but Adminius had apparently fallen out with his father shortly before the latter's death and had fled to Rome where he sought protection from the Emperor Caligula. The Romans had never relinquished their ambitions to gain a permanent foothold in Britain following the partly successful incursions of Caesar in the previous century, although Caligula was indecisive and failed to act. However, his successor Claudius was more determined and in AD 43 unleashed his legions on the ill-prepared Britons.

The Roman army landed, probably at Richborough in Kent, under the command of Aulus Plautius. The force was made up of four legions (II Augusta, XIV Gemima, IX Hispana and XX Valeria) plus the usual complement of auxiliary troops that would have swelled the ranks to some 40,000 fighting men. Their objective, of course, was the submission of the British tribes, but especially the capture of Camulodunum. The main British resistance was organised by Cunobelin's remaining sons, Togodumnus and Caractacas, who put up a determined fight near the Medway crossing which impeded the Roman advance for at least two days. Togodumnus was finally killed, although his brother escaped to fight another day. The Romans, meanwhile, proceeded to cross the Thames and enter Essex, where they halted their advance to await the arrival of their Emperor, in order that he might personally take possession of the enemy's stronghold.

Claudius, no doubt, had already departed from Rome accompanied by a large detachment of his own elite Praetorian guard, and was probably travelling at a safe distance behind the main invasion force. He was also accompanied, we are told, by a troop of armoured elephants, the sight alone of which would probably have struck terror among the native tribes, who had probably never seen such animals before. Claudius duly arrived at Camulodunum and over the next two weeks received the formal surrender of several British kings, before returning with his Praetorian guard to Rome. Upon his arrival back in Italy, he was treated as a conquering hero. The Senate awarded him a victory parade of the city, and later erected two large triumphal arches dedicated to his glorious victory, one being erected in Rome and the other possibly in Boulogne. Claudius had taken a huge personal and political gamble both in launching the invasion to start with, and then in leaving the relative safety of his home country, but it had paid off and he was now reaping the rewards.

The Roman legions remained in Britain with the XX Valeria being stationed at Camulodunum. A large legionary fortress was soon established on the site of the present-day town, which followed the usual design plan of other Roman fortresses. It covered an area of some 48 acres (*c*.20 hectares) and would have included about sixty barrack blocks, stabling for horses, stores, workshops, latrines, a hospital and various administrative buildings. Each of the barrack blocks alone would have been over 200ft long by about 60ft wide and would have provided accommodation for a century (eighty) of soldiers.

Bronze bust of the Emperor Claudius found in the river Alde, Suffolk, in 1907.

In about AD 49 the fortress was disbanded and the XX Valeria posted to another part of the country. The Romans were no doubt satisfied that this part of the country, at least, was under their control and posed no further threat. But rather than demolishing the camp altogether, they decided to convert the buildings for civilian use and establish a Roman *colonia*, or city, in which they would settle veteran soldiers retired from the Roman army. The veterans would be awarded plots of land taken from the native population with the idea of providing a Roman presence in the far-flung province. At the same time it was good way of providing a soldier with a pension after twenty-five years of faithful service. The *colonia*, which was named *Colonia Victricensis* (Colony of the Victorious) covered an area of 108 acres (44 hectares), with the old fortress being extended on its northern and eastern sides.

The Roman historian Tacitus provides us with a clue as to how the new *colonia* was developed, and to what extent the native population were dispossessed of their lands:

> What chiefly fired their [the native population's] indignation was the conduct of the veterans, lately planted as a colony at Camulodunum. These men treated the Britons with cruelty and oppression; they drove the natives from their habitations, and calling them by the opprobrious names of slaves and captives, added to their tyranny.

Tacitus was also critical of the way in which the Roman generals had neglected to provide the new colony with any defensive fortifications, preferring instead to concentrate on the provision of amenities for the enjoyment of the populace. And it was this neglect that was to have dire consequences for the colonists, as we shall later learn.

Perhaps the greatest addition to the new *colonia*, however, was the building of the great Temple of Claudius. When the Emperor Claudius died in Rome in AD 54, he was deified as a god and numerous temples dedicated to his worship were built throughout the Empire. Having decided to build such a temple in Britain, the site chosen for its erection was the new *colonia* at Camulodunum. The temple would have been comparable in size with some of the great temples in Rome itself, and would have dominated the skyline of the new colony. To the indigenous population, however, the building would have been viewed as little more than another symbol of their domination by their aggressive new masters.

Remarkably, and with a lot of help from the Norman invaders a millennium later, the foundation podium upon which the temple rested has survived and can be viewed beneath the remains of the castle. This would have been the first substantial stone and mortar building ever erected in Britain and is thus an extremely rare sur-vival from the town's early history.

A reconstruction drawing of the Balkerne Gateway area as seen from the south west.

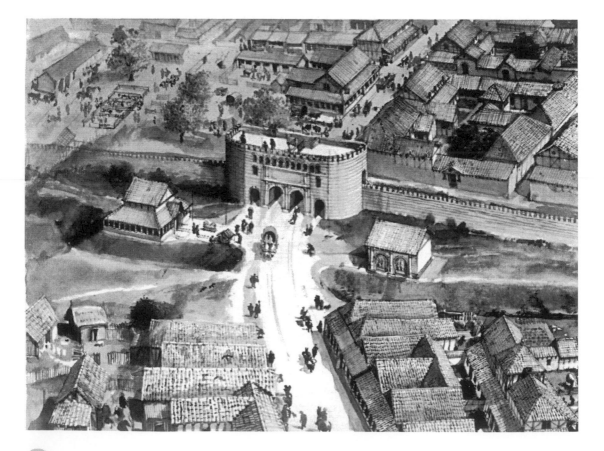

Colonia Victricensis, however, was about to enter into a new phase of activity, and one that would rock the very foundations of the new settlement. In AD 60, King Prasutagus of the Iceni tribe, who had formed an alliance with Rome, had died and his widow Boudica and two daughters had been cruelly treated by the Romans. The result was a massive uprising among the local tribes led by Boudica herself. The principal target of their hatred and vengeful spirit was the *colonia* at Camulodunum and, especially, the newly dedicated Temple of Claudius. Opinions differ as to the size of the native army, but according to the Roman historian Dio Cassius, it was at least 120,000 strong. The Roman camp at Camulodunum had, of course, been disbanded some years earlier, leaving just a small garrison of perhaps a few hundred men for its defence. The Romans attempted to halt their progress towards their new capital at Camulodunum, but it was to no avail and the Britons made swift progress covering the 80 or so miles across country.

As noted above, the Romans had given scant attention to the provision of any fortifications for their new *colonia* and appear to have adopted a rather laid-back approach to the whole affair. The result was that they were quickly overrun by the marauding Britons and their *colonia* was utterly destroyed by fire. In fact, it would appear from the remaining archaeological record that each and every building may have been systematically targeted and set ablaze. This must indeed have been a terrifying experience for the population of the *colonia* and surrounding area, which may well have totalled between 10,000 and 15,000. Tactius himself records that the colonists were totally unprepared for the onslaught and were taken by surprise. He continues that many retreated to the relative safety of the Temple where they managed to hold the Britons at bay for two days before being overwhelmed and, presumably, taken away and slaughtered. Fired by their success at Camulodunum, Boudica's army went on to deliver similar blows to the colonies at London and St Albans, before finally being thoroughly defeated after coming up against a reorganised Roman army, possibly somewhere to the north of Hertfordshire.

As far as the modern archaeologist is concerned, the Boudican attack on the town is of major importance, particularly with regard to the destruction that occurred as a result of the fire. For at virtually every site where Roman levels have been excavated in the modern town centre, there is clear evidence, often in the form of a distinctive layer of charred remains, of this terrible blaze, which of course allows the archaeologists to date their finds accurately.

Following the Boudican revolt the town was rebuilt, and the Temple of Claudius was presumably rededicated, although from this point on there does appear to have been a progressive move to transfer the administrative side of things to London, which, of course, was far better situated. But the *colonia* here at Camulodunum continued to flourish. We know from the archaeological record, especially from Roman burial sites, that a community was still thriving here well into the fourth century.

In fact, over the years, a number of tombstones and other graveyard goods have been discovered in various parts of the town, particularly along the western approaches, which is exactly where we would have expected to find them. It is well known that the Romans were not allowed to bury their dead within the confines of their walled towns or cities, and that their burial sites tended to be located on the main approach roads to the town or city (the Avenue of Tombs). This has certainly proved true in the case of Colchester. In the Castle Museum are two particularly fine Roman tombstones which have been recovered from the Lexden Road area. One of them belonged to a cavalry officer named Longinus Sdapeze, who

An imaginative reconstruction of Roman Colchester looking south east in about AD 150. The theatre can be seen in the right foreground with the Temple of Claudius in the precinct beyond.

was presumably a serving soldier at the time of his death, as the tombstone records that he had only completed fifteen years' service. The stone depicts a Roman cavalry officer on horseback, under which is a cowering Briton. Interestingly, when the stone was discovered in 1928, the face of the Roman cavalry officer was missing, whilst that of the Briton was intact. This has led to the suggestion that the tombstone may have been vandalised at the time of the Boudican revolt, and the fact that Boudica's army may well have had to pass along this Avenue of Tombs as they left Colchester en route to London gives some credence to the story. Amazingly, the missing face of the cavalry officer was discovered by James Fawn (Colchester Archaeological Group) in 1996 whilst excavating the same site where the tombstone was originally found in preparation for new building work. The face has now been reunited with its tombstone.

Another burial site in the town which has yielded some interesting finds is the so-called Butt Road cemetery, on the site of the present police station. In addition to the discovery of several hundred burials, archaeologists have uncovered the remains of an early

Street plan of Roman Colchester.

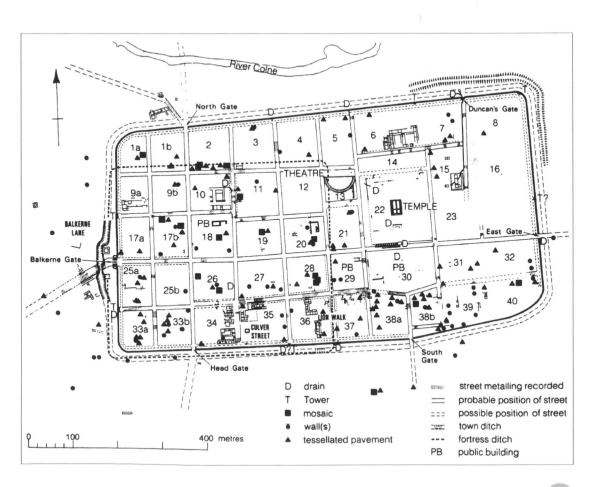

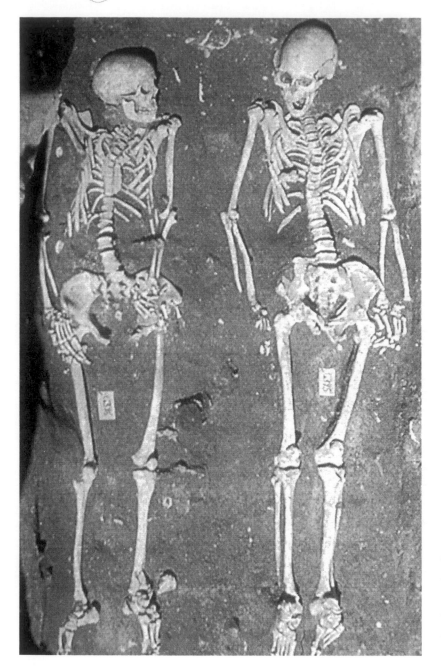

This double burial found on the site is probably that of a husband and wife who lived in Colchester during the fourth century (the female is to the right).

fourth-century Christian church, which is now on permanent display to the public. In the graveyard area itself, the diggers were amazed to discover two distinct burial periods, one overlying the other. All of the burials discovered in the upper layers of the soil were aligned in an east-west direction, the method still practised by Christians, but when they dug deeper they came across another set of burials which were all aligned in a north-south direction, after the pagan practice. This would certainly suggest that the community

that the graveyard served had adopted the Christian faith following the Emperor Constantine's decree in 313 (the Edict of Milan) that Christian worship was to be tolerated throughout the Empire. Among the burials excavated was the grave of a man and woman, probably husband and wife. The skull of the female was subsequently sent to Professor Richard Neave's forensic team at Manchester University, where they proceeded to reconstruct a lifelike model of the woman's head. The reconstructed head is now on display with the skeleton in the Castle Museum, and the woman has been named 'Camilla', after Camulodunum.

The partial remains of a fourth-century Christian church on the corner of Southway and Maldon Road. The associated cemetery is thought to have once contained several thousand graves – some Christian and some pagan.

CHAPTER 2
Saxons and Danes

Following the withdrawal of the Roman legions from Britain in the early fifth century, *Colonia Victricensis* appears to have entered a period of decline, although the process of depopulation may well have started some years earlier. Certainly the streets, buildings and monuments of the Roman town gradually fell into a state of disrepair and decay, although to what extent the former inhabitants of the surrounding area remained in place is not clear. As far as the later Saxon immigrants are concerned, it would appear that for the most part they shunned the idea of reoccupying or extensively rebuilding the Roman town, although there is some evidence of continuity of occupation. The Saxons did, however, bring to the country a new language, and probably a new name for *Colonia Victricensis*. Certainly by the late Saxon period, the town was being referred to as *Colneceaster* (possibly deriving from 'fortress on the Colne', or possibly '*colonia* fortress'). But, in reality, we know very little of what occurred in the town during the two or three centuries following the departure of the Romans.

The arrival of Anglo-Saxons settlers in Britain is supposed to have begun about 450, and certainly from the fifth and sixth centuries we can find archaeological evidence of their presence in and around Colchester. To date, three Saxon houses have been discovered within the walls of the Roman town – the earliest dating from around the mid-fifth century and the latest from the seventh century. In one of the huts a piece of broken loom-weight was found in the backfill of the hollowed-out floor, suggesting that some kind of weaving activity may have taken place here. Numerous burials associated with the Saxon period have also been recorded. These again date from the fifth and sixth centuries and have yielded numerous grave goods, including weapons, coins and jewellery.

The appearance of the town in the years following the demise of the Roman period would undoubtedly have undergone dramatic change, as the former streets of the *colonia* slowly gave way to an environment more attuned to the needs of the new inhabitants. Although some of the larger stone buildings, such the Temple of Claudius, would have survived the transition, by now a far greater percentage of available land within the walled town would have

The Saxon tower of Holy Trinity church.

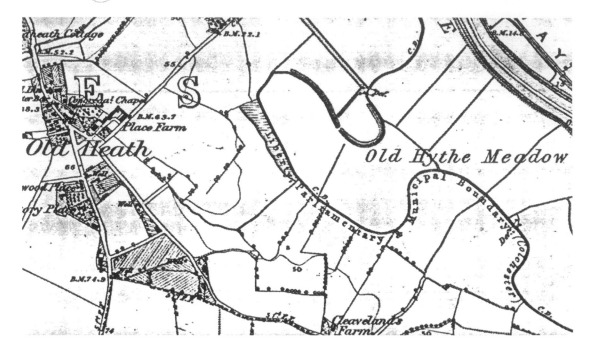

been given over to the cultivation of crops, tended by the new Saxon settlers in their small wooden houses.

And this is really about as far as it goes with regard to our knowledge of the early Saxon period – certainly as far as Colchester is concerned, it really was the Dark Ages. We have to wait until the tenth century before the town once again figures in the historical record. And for this we have to look within the pages of the *Anglo-Saxon Chronicle*, a group of documentary sources reckoned to be the most important work written in English before the Norman Conquest.

The relatively short account relating to Colchester in the *Chronicle* refers to wars with the Danes, who by the eighth century were giving the earlier Saxon settlers a taste of their own medicine, with their marauding raids along the east and south coast of England. From 865 the Danes began to settle in East Anglia and within a few years had taken control of much of the area.

Although there is no direct archaeological evidence to suggest a Danish presence in the town, we know from the *Chronicle* that the town was occupied by the Danes in the early tenth century and that they were defeated in battle by King Edward the Elder (son of Alfred the Great). The *Chronicle* states that in 917 'a great force gathered together from Kent, Surrey and Essex and marched on Colchester and surrounded the fortress and attacked until they had captured it: they slew all the inhabitants, and seized everything inside, except the men who escaped over the wall.' Later in the same

Detail from a late nineteenth-century map showing the former meandering course of the River Colne. Presumably the old Saxon harbour was located nearby.

year it was reported that 'King Edward went with the army of West Saxons to Colchester and repaired and rebuilt the fortress where it had been destroyed.' This has been taken to mean that the town walls were repaired, and could also have been the time when the town's main Roman gateway at the top of Balkerne Hill was blocked up.

Following the overthrow of the Danish garrison the town appears to have developed into a thriving Saxon settlement. Certainly the town played host to two royal councils in 931 and 940, which would suggest that the town was an important centre of administration. There is also evidence to suggest that a new port may have been constructed further downriver near to the present-day Old Heath. This name is a corruption of 'Old Hythe', which comes from the Saxon *hetha*, signifying a harbour.

By the time of the Norman Conquest the town was considered relatively prosperous, with a population of some 2,000 or more people.

CHAPTER 3
The Norman Conquest

The Norman Conquest brought mixed fortunes for the people of Colchester. For many Saxon landowners it meant ruin, as their properties were confiscated and given over to their new Norman overlords. On top of this, the town in general suffered greatly in the immediate post-conquest period from the burden of high taxation at a rate exceeded only by Rochester. On the brighter side of things, however, towards the end of the eleventh century the town finally began to prosper under the control of its baronial lord Eudo Dapifer, about whom we will hear more later.

Without doubt, the best source of information regarding this period of the town's history is the *Domesday Book*. This was also, in affect, the first national census of the country and took the form of a detailed survey of the nation's landowners, listing their respective holdings and values, both at the time of the Conquest in 1066 and in 1086. William must have felt at ease with and had some respect for the Saxon system of landholding and administration that he had inherited, as he was prepared to make full use of the system in attempting to compile an accurate valuation of his newly conquered land.

The Colchester entry in the survey is quite detailed and shows that in 1066 one of the principal inhabitants of the town was a man called Godric, who is said to have possessed four manors, 24 acres of meadow marsh, a mill, as well as a church and four hides of land (*c.*400 acres) in Greenstead. Interestingly, only one other church is mentioned in the survey, namely St Peter's on North Hill. It is highly likely, however, that there were several other churches at this time, as the survey also mentions that there were seven priests. We also know, of course, that Holy Trinity church, with its Saxon tower and doorway, must have been standing at this time. The fact that Godric is mentioned first would also imply that he was held in some esteem locally, a fact confirmed when we find him listed again in the West Donyland entry as being 'Godric of Colchester'.

The survey goes on to list the names of 276 burgesses (men holding full rights of citizenship) who between them owned around 350 houses and nearly 1,300 acres of land. In total the survey makes mention of at least 419 houses, which may suggest a total population of about 2,250, much less than the 10,000-plus population of the early Roman period.

Of the other names mentioned in the survey, one of the most prominent is Eudo de Rie (Dapifer), a Norman baron who owned five houses and 40 acres of land in Colchester. He was also privileged to serve as the royal steward, or dapifer, to the Conqueror himself as well as his sons William II and Henry I, receiving in return the lordship of at least sixty-four manors in the eastern counties of England. But it is in Colchester where he is remembered as a great benefactor, and the man responsible for carrying out a number of important building projects, including the castle and St John's Abbey.

Colchester Castle is one of the town's great legacies from the Norman period. According to a fourteenth-century document known as the *Colchester Chronicle* it was built by Eudo himself in 1076. The *Chronicle*, however, is known to contain several textual errors, and so cannot always be relied upon as a statement of fact. For one thing, we know that the castle was from the beginning a royal fortress and not a baronial one, and as such it seems rather unlikely that it would have been built by a mere baron – unless, of course, he was building it on behalf of the king. The position is further complicated by another passage in the *Chronicle* which states that 'King William the Younger gave to Eudo the town of Colchester, with the castle, to possess in perpetuity' in 1089. This would imply that before this the castle was in the possession of the Crown. The earliest source independent of the *Chronicle* which throws further light on the matter is a charter of Henry I (1101) granting to Eudo the town of Colchester and the '*turrim* and *castellum*', which would seem to refer to both the 'keep' and the 'castle', or surrounding fortifications,

An imaginative reconstruction of Norman Colchester showing the castle and defensive earthworks.

suggesting that perhaps only part of the castle complex had been completed at the earlier period. So it is not clear whether Eudo had been responsible for building the castle in the first place, as recorded in the *Colchester Chronicle*, or whether he had simply been granted the building at a later date. But whatever the truth of the matter, the charter of 1101 seems to provide a date by which building work on the castle had been completed.

The present castle keep was certainly one of the first Norman keeps in the country to be built entirely from stone, and has the distinction of being the largest Norman keep ever constructed. It is similar in design to the White Tower in London, which suggests that both buildings may have been the work of Gandulf, Bishop of Rochester, who is known to have designed the White Tower. But there the similarity ends, for the keep at Colchester was constructed mainly from recycled Roman brick and stone taken from the old town. Furthermore, the entire structure rests upon the foundation podium of the old Roman temple of Claudius, which had been constructed over a thousand years earlier. It is interesting to note that the passage in the *Colchester Chronicle* stating that the castle was built by Eudo in 1076 also mentions that it was built on the foundation of King Coel's palace. Now the *Chronicle* also mentions that King Coel, the father of St Helena, built his city here and reigned over Essex and Hertfordshire in the early third century. Perhaps Coel had indeed built a palace here on the site of the Roman temple and that it was this building that the Normans discovered above ground when they arrived after the Conquest, rather than the temple itself.

Following Eudo's death in 1120 the castle reverted to the Crown, in whose hands it remained almost without exception for the next 500 or so years before being sold into private ownership. But one question still remains unanswered after all these years: what exactly did the castle look like?. In particular, how high was the building? In the past, a popular theory was that the building was originally four storeys high, a notion based on little more than a comparison with the Tower of London. Certainly the present two-storey structure has been reduced in height, but to what extent is unknown. We know that the building was purchased by John Wheely in 1683 with the aim of pulling it down and selling off the resulting spoil at a profit. The historian Philip Morant, in his *History of Colchester* of 1748, makes it clear that this is exactly what Wheely began to do: 'the tops of the towers and walls were forced down with screws, or blown up with gunpowder, and thrown upon the heads of the arched vaults below'. What Morant does not say, how-

ever, is exactly how much of the walls were removed. It could have been 40ft or more, or perhaps as little as a few inches. It may be that the original plans for a three- or four-storey castle were never implemented in full, and that what we see today may be similar to what Wheely bought in 1683.

Eudo Dapifer was also responsible for the building of St John's Abbey, a wealthy Benedictine monastery which remained a prominent force in the town's history until the reign of Henry VIII. The abbey was founded in 1095 by Eudo and subsequently endowed with scores of manors, church tithes and numerous other benefits, which included the restored chapel of St Helen with 14 acres of land, and the right to hold an annual fair on St John's Green. The abbots of the monastery were also privileged to wear the mitred hat of a bishop and to have a seat in the House of Lords. Unfortunately nothing whatsoever remains of the abbey building itself, save the late fifteenth-century gatehouse which today stands as a poignant reminder of former times.

The abbey is said to have been built on a site where a priest or holy man named Siric had a small house and church. This church, apparently dedicated to St John the Evangelist, was built of timber, with planking for its walls. Tradition also asserts that the site was known as a place where miracles had taken place, where strange lights had been seen, and where inexplicable voices were often heard. The fact many people are said to have testified to such happenings was probably enough for Eudo to choose the site for his monastery. And, bearing in mind that the abbey was founded within just ten years of the Domesday survey, one may also wonder whether this Siric was in fact one of the seven Colchester priests mentioned in the survey.

Eudo Dapifer, the Norman ruler of Colchester.

The stone keep of Colchester Castle can be seen on the right of this sixteenth-century view of Colchester.

The abbey was completed by 1115, but following the strict rules of the Benedictine order, permission to worship in the abbey church was not afforded to the general public, who instead had to use St Giles' church, which was built in 1171. Eudo had also decreed that upon his death his body was to be laid to rest within the abbey, and although he died at his castle in Préaux in Normandy, his body was returned to Colchester for burial in accordance with his wishes.

Within a few years of a start being made on St John's Abbey, the town was blessed with yet another religious house in the form of St Botolph's Priory. This is said to have been founded by a local clergyman called Ernulph (Ainulf), who, it seems, had charge of a small company of priests attached to an existing church of the same dedication. These priests, after deciding to adopt monastic orders, sent two of their number to France, where they studied the rules of the Augustinian canons. When they returned to England the priory was established under Augustinian rules, and in due course received a charter of protection from William Rufus. This dates the foundation of the priory, the first house of Augustinian canons in England, to some time before that king's death in 1100. Ernulph became its first prior, a position he held until 1116.

As at most houses of the Augustinian order, and in contrast to the arrangements already noted at St John's Abbey, there did exist at St Botolph's an agreement with the general populace allowing them to make use of the priory church for public worship. This special privi-

An eighteenth-century view of the castle, with its owner Charles Gray (cane in hand) and friends in the foreground.

lege may have been connected in some way with a continuation of previous rights, already established within the community under the earlier church. The most striking difference between the two houses, however, was a monetary one, for the priory was never to become a wealthy house in the same league as St John's, which is one reason, perhaps, why it took over seventy years to build.

The only known drawing of St John's Abbey.

One other notable work of the great Eudo before his death in 1120 was the founding of a leper hospital on the outskirts of the town leading to the Hythe. The hospital was dedicated to St Mary Magdalene and provided accommodation for a master and four leprous persons. This is indeed a stark reminder of the former prevalence of this terrible disease, which would have been very familiar to the population of the time. Some years after Eudo's death, a charter of Henry II granted the income from the manor of Brightlingsea to St John's Abbey, on condition that £6 a year thereof was used for looking after the inmates of the hospital. The hospital was therefore placed under the charge of the abbey, which provided the lepers with a daily allowance of bread, beer and meat.

The town would undoubtedly have benefited from the presence of these two religious houses, especially St John's, which would have provided work and contracts for quite a large number of people. But we still know very little about life in the town during this post–Conquest period. Our best source of evidence, as noted above, is the

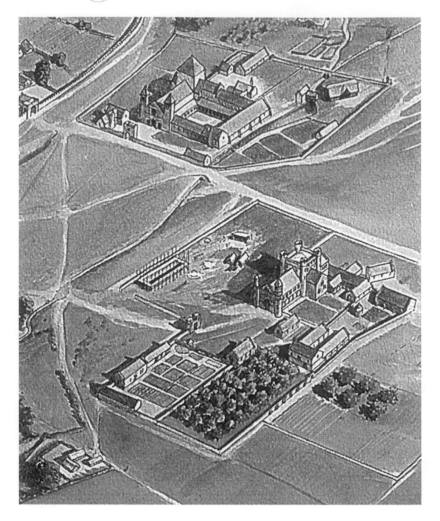

An imaginative reconstruction of Norman Colchester showing St Botolph's Priory (top) and St John's Abbey (below).

Domesday survey itself, which paints a fairly clear picture of what life in the town revolved around. Despite having borough status and being an urban and market centre for the surrounding communities, life in the town still appeared to revolve very much around the agricultural calendar. For example, of the 276 burgesses mentioned in the survey, over 50 per cent held several acres of land in addition to their property holdings, providing an indication of their lifestyle and source of income. We also know from a grant made to the burgesses during the reign of Henry II (1154–89) that they enjoyed the right of regular commoning, or grazing, upon several hundred acres of land around the town, a privilege which they jealously guarded for centuries afterwards. For the final word on the matter, however, we must return once again to St John's Abbey and to an illuminating passage in one of its early chronicles. Here we find what is perhaps the first general description of the town written during the post-Conquest period:

The city of Colchester is placed in the eastern part of Britain, a city near to a port, pleasantly situated, watered on every side with abundant springs, with a very healthy air, built with very strong walls; a city to be reckoned among the most eminent, had not time, fires, floods, incursions of pirates, and various strokes of misfortune obliterated all the monuments of the city.

St Botolph's Priory as it may have once appeared.

CHAPTER 4
The Medieval Borough

The town's first royal charter was granted by Richard I in 1189 as he was preparing to depart on the Third Crusade. It granted to the burgesses of Colchester the rights to self-government, to choose their own administration and judicial officers, and to claim exemption from all other courts and jurisdictions in the land. Interestingly, the wording of the charter makes clear that the king was actually 'granting and confirming' these privileges, an indication that the town had already become a self-contained borough some time before this date, with the right to hold its own courts etc. Other rights granted and confirmed to the burgesses included the right to hunt the fox, hare and cat (polecat) within the liberties of the borough, and to have control of the fisheries of the River Colne from North Bridge to Westnesse. The value of this latter privilege was enhanced by the inclusion of the many creeks and tributaries of the River Colne, which contain some of the finest oyster beds in the area, and although in the Middle Ages oysters were probably of less value than fish, they were nevertheless an important part of most people's diet and were sold freely in the market place.

In medieval times the right to become a burgess of the town, and to benefit from the numerous privileges embodied in successive royal charters, could be claimed by anyone who had been born in the town, provided that they could find two existing burgesses to sponsor them. Sons and grandsons of burgesses could also claim the right, as could those who had served a seven-year apprenticeship with an existing burgess. Those born outside the borough (foreigners) could also claim burgess status upon payment of a sum of money, known as a fine. In later periods the burgesses became known as 'free burgesses' and later still 'freemen'.

The benefits of being a burgess were numerous and in addition to those mentioned above, it gave the recipient the right to trade in the borough without hindrance or payment of any tolls or fines. They were allowed to graze the commons (known as half-year lands) for six months of each year between August and February, and to receive a share of any corporate income raised through toll charges, rents, fines, or by any other means. But perhaps of particular

Detail from a royal charter granted to the burgesses of Colchester by Henry V in 1413. It incorporates the figures of St Helena and her son Constantine the Great, and includes the earliest known representation of the borough's coat of arms.

importance, to some at least, was the right to have a say in the corporate running of the town and to vote in elections.

Colchester remained an important town and trading centre throughout the medieval period. It was the largest town in Essex and by around 1300 had a population of between 3,000 and 4,000. One of the best sources for gaining a better understanding of the town's financial position and how the people lived and earned their living is the surviving taxation subsidies. These subsidies, or lay subsidies as they were often known (i.e. the clergy were generally not included), were a way of raising money for a specific purpose such as fighting a foreign war. In most cases, and particularly between 1290 and 1334, a person was taxed on his movable goods only (both household and stock in trade) rather than on his land or property. The taxes were commonly known as the 'tenth' or the 'fifteenth' based on the rate of tax which was levied. The lists are particularly informative and usually provide information regarding occupation and details of household goods and other movable possessions belonging to the individuals concerned.

In the twenty-ninth year of the reign of Edward I (1300–01) the inhabitants of Colchester were obliged to pay a tax based on a fifteenth of the value of their movable goods. Detailed inventories were drawn up providing information on the kind of homes in which they lived, together with a list of their taxable possessions and value. A total of 390 persons were named in the subsidy, which

included both rich and poor alike. In fact, nobody escaped the asses-
sors' probing investigations. For example, John Fitz-elias, a poor
weaver, whose goods and chattels amounted to just one old coat valued at 2s and one lamb valued at 6d, had to pay a 'fifteenth' tax of 2d.
At the other end of the scale we find people such as Henry P'son
(Pearson), who was one of the wealthiest men assessed, and who was
taxed on movable goods worth £5 3s 1d. His inventory lists the kind
of personal possessions which he no doubt deemed to be of value, as
well as showing that that even in the case of a man of considerable
wealth, he actually had very little in way of household goods or
other possessions. His entire inventory reads as follows:

> 1 gold buckle 14d; and gold ring 12d; 2 silver spoons 16d; a cup 14d;
> 2 gowns 10s; 1 mappa and 2 towels 2s 6d; 2 beds 5s; 1 mantell ½
> mark, 1 brass olla 2s; 1 brass dish 22d; a washing basin and ewer
> [*lotor cum pelvi*] 14d; 2qt barley at 3s; 3qt oats at 2s; 1 ox carcass 4s;
> sepum 2s; pinguedo 2s; 1 piece russet cloth 9s; 3lb wool 3s; 2 horses
> 1 mark, hay 2s; 1 cart 4s; wood and faggots 2s; 2 barrels 9d; cuvas
> algeas et cuvell, 2s 2d; 1 trivit, 1 andiron, 1 candlestick 12d; Total
> £5 3s 1d.

Apart from just one or two items of gold and silver, and a map, it
would appear that he had very little in the way of personal possessions. Note also that his two gowns, valued at 10s, were worth twice
as much as his two beds, and almost as much as his two horses
(1 mark = 13s 4d).

The inventories are also useful in providing us with an idea of the
kind of houses in which people lived. Generally speaking, the living
accommodation for the average person or family would have been
quite small, comprising just a living room (the hall), a kitchen and a
chamber (withdrawing room cum bedroom), all of which would
have been sparsely furnished by modern standards. And, as shown
above, even the wealthiest inhabitants of the town appear to have
had very little in the way of household furniture or personal
belongings, when compared to a typical household of today.

The returns can also be used for gaining information on the
numerous occupations and trades that the people were engaged in.
For example, the return of 1301 shows that thirteen people were
working in the tanning business – in fact, the most highly taxed man
in the town was a tanner named Henry Pakeman who had movable
goods valued at nearly £10. And a further seventeen people were
assessed on leather and shoes, an indication perhaps of the main use
to which the raw leather was put. Other trades mentioned include

cutlers, goldsmiths, glass workers, vintners and several occupations allied to the wool trade such as weavers, dyers, fullers and wool-combers. However, the chief kind of movable wealth assessed across the board was in some way connected with agriculture, which shows that despite the fairly extensive trade in tanning and leather work, and the emerging cloth industry, this still remained the dominant form of occupation and trade.

The River Colne and harbour area from an eighteenth-century drawing.

The town's port at the Hythe was also developing at this time, having been established a few years earlier at a new site a short distance upriver from the old Saxon port at Old Hythe (Old Heath). This became known as New Hythe and by the late fourteenth century had been provided with extensive wharves and warehousing, as well as two cranes which are believed to have been among the earliest known in England. Trade was apparently brisk and between February 1397 and February 1398 the port was visited by thirty-two ships engaged in overseas trade. Imports included such things as wheat, bitumen, timber, beer, fish, wine and various other manufactured goods and commodities, while exports included cloth, hides, butter and cheese. The record also shows that at the time of the blockade of Calais (1346–47) during the Hundred Years' War with France, the town was called upon to provide five ships and 170 mariners, which is another indication of the relative prosperity of

Detail of the Hythe community showing Hythe Hill and St Leonard's church. Although viewed from an eighteenth-century perspective, it provides us with a flavour of the medieval port.

the port at this time. It is also likely that the ships themselves would have been built along the banks of the Colne, thereby giving rise to yet another industry.

Shortly after this, the first of several outbreaks of plague dealt a devastating blow to the people of this country. This first visitation, the most virulent, has come to be known as the Black Death. The disease is believed to have originated in the plains of central Asia in the 1330s and by 1349 had ravaged most of Europe. It has been estimated that between a third and a half of the population of the country may have succumbed to the disease, which eventually led to the depopulation of as many as 1,000 villages.

The plague is thought to have reached Colchester early in 1349 and lingered on until the autumn. There is little surviving evidence, however, to suggest how many people perished as a result of the disease, but estimates of between 1,000 and 1,500 may not be too far out. Certainly the mortality rate in the town was far higher than normal during this period, judging by the large number of wills which were proved in the borough court between September 1348 and September 1349 – more than fifty times the normal number.

We also have little knowledge as to how the population in general was affected. Whether the disease struck young and old alike, or tended towards a particular class of society, is not clear. We do know, however, that both the abbot and prior of St John's were probably both dead by August 1348 – possibly as a result of the plague. Further outbreaks occurred later in the fourteenth century, and the disease was to remain endemic in this country until the late seventeenth century.

Despite the many setbacks that must have occurred during those ill-fated years, the town was to experience a sustained recovery in the years which followed. This was due, in part, to a steady flow of immigrants and others who had been attracted to the town's steadily growing cloth industry. The population thus quickly recovered and in 1377 a total of 2,951 people in the town are known to have paid a poll tax, resulting in Colchester being listed as the eighth largest provincial town in England, and suggesting a total population of between 4,000 and 5,000. This represents a population increase of around 25 per cent over the previous sixty-five years, even allowing for the decimations of the plague years.

The next major event of concern to have left its mark on the town's history was the Peasants' Revolt of 1381. The insurgence took the form of a general uprising among the peasant classes of the country, who for many years had been nurturing a great deal of hatred and resentment about their lot in life. In general terms, the working people at this time had been reduced to living a life of near slavery. They had few rights and nearly every aspect of their down-trodden lives was designed to benefit their lords and masters.

It was thus against this background of inequality between rich and poor that the government decided to impose a succession of crippling poll taxes to support the ongoing wars with France, and which was to become a catalyst for rebellion. For unlike previous taxations, or subsidies, where a person was taxed according to his

St Helen's chapel before its late nineteenth-century restoration.

Detail from an eighteenth-century view of the north prospect of Colchester, showing part of the Dutch Quarter.

individual wealth (or at least his movable wealth), the poll taxes exacted the same amount of payment across the board, regardless of status. The first of these taxes took place in 1377 when a tax of one groat (4d) was levied on every lay person above the age of fourteen. This was followed in 1379 with another tax based on the payment of one groat, although on this occasion graduating upwards according to status. But then in 1381 came the most crippling tax of all. Everyone above the age of fifteen had to pay a tax of three groats (1s) which for most people would have represented about three days' wages. The result was that the poorest in the land contributed the same amount as the wealthiest – a blatant injustice which only served to fuel the fires of discontent.

The people of Essex were among the first to rise in revolt, spurred on by the revolutionary preaching and doctrines of men like John Ball who held the position of parochial chaplain at St James's church in Colchester. In fact, Ball went on to become one the leaders of the revolt, along with Wat Tyler and others, and was hotly pursued by the authorities for a number of weeks before being arrested in Coventry on 13 July 1381. He is perhaps best remembered, however, for his celebrated sermon on Blackheath Common on 13 June, when he emphasised the fact that in God's eyes all men were equal, and that it was only as a result of the hard labours of the poor that the rich were able to lead their privileged lifestyles. After his arrest he was taken to St Albans and put on trial. He admitted inciting others to rebel and was subsequently condemned to be hanged, drawn and quartered. He was executed in the presence of the king and several of his ministers in a public square near St Albans on 15 July.

Although Colchester had been one of the first towns to fall to the rebels, the town managed to escape any serious trouble. However, on the day following Wat Tyler's death in London on 15 June, the rebels did launch an attack on the Moot Hall and threatened to burn the borough muniments and court rolls, apparently anxious to destroy any incriminating evidence while they had the chance. Unusually, one of the rioters was a man named William atte Appleton, who was a fuller and a burgess of the town. He was subsequently arrested and brought before the borough court on 4 October, where he was charged with the offence and remanded in prison. On 23 October he was tried and found guilty of the charge, but, no doubt having several friends in high places, managed to avoid a prison sentence upon payment of a fine of half a mark (6s 8d). The fact that men such as Appleton are known to have risked their livelihoods and freedom by engaging in such riotous behaviour adds weight to the view held by some that the revolt extended well beyond the peasant classes of society.

Yet another disturbance took place on 30 September when the rebels made a further attack on the Moot Hall, and also on St John's Abbey. Again the rioters threatened to burn the court records in the

The old Moot Hall.

Moot Hall, but apparently failed to do so. The monks of St John's, however, were not so lucky and the rioters successfully carried off and burnt a number of court rolls belonging to the manors of Greenstead and West Donyland.

And yet despite having to live through these troublesome times, Colchester emerged relatively unscathed. As noted above, this was probably due in large part to the rapidly growing cloth industry in England, whose fruits Colchester was well placed to enjoy. Wool was freely available from sheep on the Essex marshes and in other neighbouring counties, and the River Colne provided the power for the fulling mills needed for the finishing processes.

The industry in Colchester really started to gain momentum in the early 1350s. This was when, in the aftermath of the Black Death, large numbers of immigrants, including many Flemish workers, settled in the town to work in this fast-growing industry. And it was the cloth trade that was to prove the making of Colchester for the next four or five hundred years, as people from all walks of society worked together to achieve a common goal – to produce as many bales of cloth as possible.

It has been estimated that the labour of as many as fifty people may have been required in the production of each bale of cloth, ranging from wool staplers, carders, woolcombers, spinners, dyers, weavers, fullers, roughers, shearers and pressers, all of whom played a vital role in the production process. And we can add to this group the clothiers themselves and numerous other individuals employed in administration. At the height of the industry locally, in the mid-fifteenth century when something in the order of 40,000 bales were being exported annually, it would have been providing work for tens of thousands of people, both in Colchester and in the surrounding villages.

For the most part, Colchester specialised in the production of a type of broadcloth known as russet, which in the fourteenth century did not necessarily imply a reddish-brown coloured cloth as might be expected today, but rather a shade varying somewhere between grey and brown. Although various types of russet were manufactured, what became universally known as 'Colchester russet' was aimed at the middle range of the market and was often purchased by the clergy.

Colchester russet was also distinctive in size, being less than half the length of a standard English broadcloth of more than 28 yards, and was known as a decena. The cloth was also manufactured in two widths, either one or two yards wide, although the narrow type, often known as 'straights', were the more popular. Narrow cloths were far easier for the weavers to work up as it was very time-consuming for a single weaver to continually pass a shuttle through a cloth two yards wide without any assistance.

By the early fifteenth century the town's trade was dominated by Hanseatic merchants. Most of the finished cloth by this time was being exported to such faraway places as Gascony, Prussia and the countries of the Mediterranean.

The cloth trade, and indeed the population of the town, reached their medieval peak around the 1440s. From hereon there was a gradual decline in numbers which continued through to the early sixteenth century, before falling at an even faster rate. By the 1520s the population of the town had fallen from a high of nearly 8,000 in 1400 to less than 5,000. Even so the town was still ranked as the eleventh largest in England, and remained one of the largest cloth-making towns in the eastern counties. However, the decline continued and numbers fell even further; the number of people taking the Oath of Allegiance in 1534 suggests that the total population had reduced to less than 4,000. Hereafter, however, the general trend was for growth and over the next 150 years the population of the town slowly recovered and by the 1660s had risen to above 10,000.

CHAPTER 5
Religious Upheavals

Life in Colchester throughout much of the sixteenth century was blighted in one way or another by religious upheaval and strife. Much, of course, depended on whose side you happened to be on at the time, but persecution for one's religious persuasion was rife and many were to suffer the ultimate penalty for their beliefs. The change to the country's religious structure began in the 1530s with the Dissolution of the Monasteries and other religious institutions, and was to have a major effect on the stability and structure of society. Then within a few years came the terrible persecutions of the reign of Queen Mary, when hundreds of people, including many from Colchester, were forced to struggle with their consciences in the face of a most cruel fate. It was not until the reign of Elizabeth I that things finally start to settle down and the country was able to enter into a period of relative peace and security.

The fires of Protestantism had been smouldering in Colchester long before the time of the Reformation. As early as 1428 we find that a tailor by the name of William Cheveling had been arrested in Colchester on the charge of heresy (i.e. for daring to question the Roman faith) and committed to prison. The bailiffs of the town wasted little time in seeking a 'writ for burning' from the king, which was duly delivered. The writ stated that the unfortunate Cheveling was to be committed to the fire in a suitably public place, and that the reason for his burning was to be publicly announced as a clear example to all Christians. He was subsequently committed to the stake and burnt at Colking's Castle (near Balkerne Gate) on the first Thursday after the Feast of All Saints in November 1428.

The death of William Cheveling appears to have quelled any similar opposition in the town for a number of years and it was not until around 1500 that opposition to the Roman Church saw something of a revival. The records show that in 1511 two Colchester heretics were burnt at Smithfield, and in 1527 a large heretical group was active in north-east Essex, including nineteen men and fourteen women from Colchester, many of whom were from the higher levels of society. They held meetings in private houses where they would preach their doctrines and read from John Wycliffe's English translation of the Bible, which was contrary to the law of the land at the time (the Bible being considered too dangerous a book for ordinary people to read).

The passing of the Act of Supremacy in 1534 confirmed the break with Rome and legitimised Henry VIII's position as the Supreme Head of the Church of England. It was followed by a series of statutes which permanently altered the beliefs and religious practices of the entire nation. Foremost among these changes was the king's decision to dissolve the monasteries and sell off their land and property. By 1540 all of the monastic houses in England and Wales had been closed.

The first of the larger monastic houses in Colchester to be dissolved was St Botolph's Priory, which was closed in 1536. However, because of the priory's former agreement with the citizens of Colchester, whereby they had been allowed to worship within the confines of the priory, the house was saved from total ruin with the priory church being allowed to remain as a place for public worship. The revenues of the house were granted to the Lord Chancellor, Sir Thomas Audley, as were those of the smaller house of the Crouched Friars.

St John's Abbey, which had managed to survive the first round of closures as a result of its higher status and value, was finally closed in 1539. However, the closure failed to proceed as smoothly as expected owing to the rebellious act of its last abbot Thomas Marshall (alias John Beche). Apparently Abbot Marshall had stubbornly refused to hand over his abbey to the king and was subsequently arrested for treason. According to a local tradition cited by the historian Philip

St John's Abbey gatehouse.

Morant in 1748, in order to arrest the abbot, the magistrates had invited him to a feast in the town and it was only when he was there among them, tucking into his meal, that they informed him of his death warrant and took him off and hanged him without further warning or ceremony. Although parts of this story may contain some elements of fact, the abbot was actually afforded a proper trial and indeed spent some time imprisoned in the Tower of London. Some reports suggest that at this stage his courage failed him and that he began to repent of his actions, saying that he would have given up his abbey rather than invoke the king's displeasure. However, he apparently held fast to his original convictions and was later returned to Colchester, where he was tried before a special commission consisting of the Earl of Essex and several other leading judges. After being found guilty of the charges against him, he was condemned and executed by hanging on 1 December 1539. The monks of St John's were granted small pensions, while the abbey itself passed into the hands of the Crown. A few years later, however, the site was leased to Sir Thomas Darcy, and later still to the Lucas family, who converted the site into a family home.

It would appear that the people of Colchester willingly accepted the principles of reform, perhaps more so than many other similar

Abbot Thomas Marshall (alias Beche) of St John's Abbey being led to the gallows for execution.

sized towns in the country. Church plate and other goods were quickly sold, and there was a swift decline in the value and number of bequests made to the church, as more people gave directly to the poor. Many religious shrines were dismantled, stone altars removed and other images and statues, viewed by the authorities as superstitious, destroyed. This extended to images on stained-glass windows and particularly wall paintings, which were whitewashed over. In fact, for many communities in the country, including Colchester, hostility to the doctrines and beliefs of the Roman Catholic Church had been deeply embedded for many years, even back to the days of John Wycliffe, who has been regarded by many as being the 'Morning Star of the Reformation'.

Obviously, at that time such heretical views would have found little support with the monks at St John's, and indeed in 1429 the abbot is said to have accused the town of being a hotbed of Lollardy, after a number Colchester men were accused of being involved in an abortive Lollard plot to take over the kingdom. But now, in the sixteenth century, views that may once have been considered heretical were now being propagated by the government itself.

It was not be long, however, before these newly acquired beliefs and doctrines of the Reformation were to be put to the severest of tests. In 1553 the Catholic Queen Mary Tudor succeeded her half-brother Edward VI to the throne and immediately set about trying to reverse the effects of the Reformation. To this end on 28 February 1554 Mary's favourite bishop, Edmund Bonner, issued an order to all his clergy to notify their parishioners that if they did not attend confession or receive the sacrament by 6 April they would be liable to prosecution. The result was that during the course of the next three or four years, some forty people from the town are known to have suffered the death penalty for their steadfast adherence to their beliefs. Most were burnt at the stake, some in London and other places, but nearly half of that number in Colchester itself, either within the Castle Bailey or outside the Balkerne Gate. The burnings always took place in front of large crowds, who would often gather to voice their support for the condemned with shouts and cries of encouragement.

The first burning in Colchester took place on 29 March 1555 when a priest by the name of John Laurence was condemned to the fire whilst sitting in a chair, he being unable to stand as a result of being severely weakened by his captors. According to an account contained in John Foxe's *Book of Martyrs,* as Laurence was sitting in the fire a number of young children came close to him and offered words of support.

The town had become one of the focal points of opposition to Mary's government. So much so that in December 1557 a Catholic priest named Tye wrote that 'the rebels are stout in the town of Colchester. The ministers of the church are hemmed in on the streets and called knaves; the blessed sacrament of the alter is blasphemed and rallied upon in every house and tavern; prayer and fasting are not regarded.' One of these rebels was a man named George Eagles (nicknamed Trudgeover), who was a tailor and itinerant preacher. He was apparently successful in avoiding the authorities for some time before finally being spotted at St Mary Magdalen Fair in 1557 and subsequently hunted down and arrested. He was later hanged, drawn and quartered at Chelmsford, after which one of his quarters was sent to Colchester to be put on display in the market place.

Also about this time a group of fourteen Protestant men and eight women from the Colchester area were arrested and tied together with rope before being driven to London like a flock of sheep, where they were imprisoned. However, their ordeal obviously

The burning of John Lawrence on 29 March 1555. This was the first death of many Protestant martyrs which took place in Colchester during the bloody reign of Queen Mary.

proving too much for them, and faced with the prospect of being burnt alive, they recanted their beliefs and submitted to the Catholic Church.

However, most of those arrested on similar charges remained firm to the end and, of the many reports cited by Foxe, the following is typical. On 2 August 1557, between six and seven o'clock in the morning, three men and three women were led from the prison in the Moot Hall to a place just outside the town wall to be burnt at the stake. After the condemned had spent sometime in prayer, and they were being prepared for the fire, one of their number, a young girl named Elizabeth Folkes, took off her petticoat and tried to hand it to her mother who had come close to kiss her daughter. However, some of those in attendance would not let her have it, so Elizabeth threw it away saying, 'Farewell all the world, farewell faith and farewell hope.' After all six had been chained to the stake, and the fire set alight, they clapped their hands together with joy in the flames, so that the crowds in attendance (numbering in their thousands) cried out with such words of encouragement as 'Lord strengthen them' and 'Lord comfort them' as they gave up their bodies to the flames.

Protestants being burned at the stake in Colchester.

The main reasons for the arrests and deaths of so many seemingly devout individuals was their universal refusal to accept the Catholic doctrine of transubstantiation (the actual presence of Christ in the sacrament), for denying the infallibility of the Pope, for refusing to worship the Virgin Mary and other saints, and for continuing to read their English Bibles.

Following Mary's death in 1558, the authorities in Colchester exercised extreme caution with regard to numerous other people whom they were still holding on suspicion of supporting convicted men like George Eagles. It was not until the day before Elizabeth's coronation that all but one of these prisoners of conscience were released from custody. Now that Elizabeth was on the throne it was the turn of the Catholics to be worried, but her anti-Catholic policies were not as extreme as her sister's persecution of Protestants. Elizabeth did, of course, re-establish Protestantism as the country's official religion, but she tended to execute only those Catholics who were a threat to her.

It was not until the reign of Charles I and, in particular, the appointment of William Laud as Archbishop of Canterbury in 1633 that further changes in matters of religion began to take place, much to the annoyance of those holding strong Puritan views. Archbishop Laud was of the opinion that the reform of the Church had probably gone too far, and in order to turn the tide as it were he brought

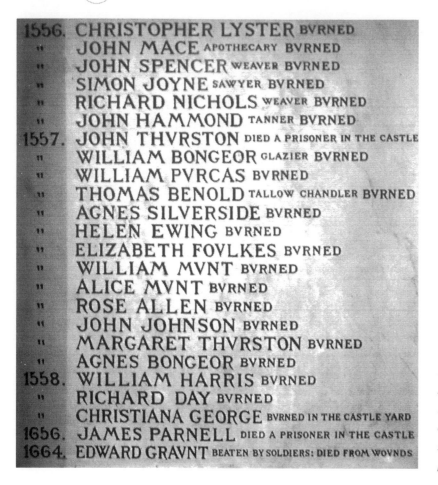

1556.	CHRISTOPHER LYSTER		BVRNED
"	JOHN MACE	APOTHECARY	BVRNED
"	JOHN SPENCER	WEAVER	BVRNED
"	SIMON JOYNE	SAWYER	BVRNED
"	RICHARD NICHOLS	WEAVER	BVRNED
"	JOHN HAMMOND	TANNER	BVRNED
1557.	JOHN THVRSTON		DIED A PRISONER IN THE CASTLE
"	WILLIAM BONGEOR	GLAZIER	BVRNED
"	WILLIAM PVRCAS		BVRNED
"	THOMAS BENOLD	TALLOW CHANDLER	BVRNED
"	AGNES SILVERSIDE		BVRNED
"	HELEN EWING		BVRNED
"	ELIZABETH FOVLKES		BVRNED
"	WILLIAM MVNT		BVRNED
"	ALICE MVNT		BVRNED
"	ROSE ALLEN		BVRNED
"	JOHN JOHNSON		BVRNED
"	MARGARET THVRSTON		BVRNED
"	AGNES BONGEOR		BVRNED
1558.	WILLIAM HARRIS		BVRNED
"	RICHARD DAY		BVRNED
"	CHRISTIANA GEORGE		BVRNED IN THE CASTLE YARD
1656.	JAMES PARNELL		DIED A PRISONER IN THE CASTLE
1664.	EDWARD GRAVNT		BEATEN BY SOLDIERS: DIED FROM WOVNDS

Detail from the Martyrs' Memorial in the Town Hall, showing the names of some of those who suffered the ultimate penalty for their beliefs.

in a series of adjustments to procedure and new regulations. For one thing, he did not like to see the altar being moved around so much, so he decreed that it was to be returned to its pre-Reformation position at the east end of the sanctuary. He also ordered that the altar should be enclosed within a series of rails at which the communicants would have to kneel. Previously, of course, since the time of the Reformation, the alter had been placed in the middle of the chancel, or even in the body of the church itself, where those taking communion could kneel directly in front of it. The railings themselves were also to be placed close together so that, according to Laud, 'dogges should not defile ye sanctuary'. And while these changes may have appeased the supporters of the High Church party, those among the large band of Puritans in the country believed that this was merely a ploy to try to reintroduce Roman ideas. And, of course, anyone found guilty of non-compliance with the new regulations would have been severely dealt with.

Nevertheless, the Protestant people of Colchester were not easily intimidated and a number of clergy and churchwardens refused to

rail in their altars. One such example occurred at St Botolph's where
James Wheeler, one of the churchwardens, refused to rail in his altar
at the command of the archdeacon. Wheeler was twice excommuni-
cated, and after still refusing to comply with the order, was thrown
into prison where he remained for three years. At some stage, however, he apparently managed to escape, and the mayor of the town,
after searching his house without authority, had his wife and children thrown into gaol in his place. After being thus confined for
three days they were released upon payment of a heavy fine.
Wheeler's wife later complained to Parliament about the way that
she had been treated and was awarded substantial damages amount-
ing to £300 (worth perhaps £30,000 today), on the basis that there
had been no official law compelling the railing-in of the communion table.

One positive outcome of the religious upheavals of the sixteenth
century was the revitalisation of the town's decaying cloth trade.
This came about as a result of yet another round of religious persecution, this time inflicted on the Protestant population of the Low
Countries – in particular, Flanders – by their Spanish rulers. The
result was that many Flemings decided to leave their homes and seek
refuge in the relative safety of England across the Channel. They
eventually settled in quite large numbers in several towns of the
eastern counties, including Colchester, whose rulers were more than
willing to accommodate them – for these were no ordinary
refugees, but rather people who knew a thing or two about cloth-
making.

The first group of fifty-five refugees (eleven families) arrived in
Colchester in 1565 and over the next few years were followed by
many others. By 1571 their numbers had risen to 185, by 1573 to
431 and by 1586 to 1,291. Their particular expertise in cloth-
making extended to the production of the so-called 'new
draperies', a superior light-weight cloth of the best quality, and in a
far higher league than that being made by the English clothiers.
The cloths which they manufactured were known as bays, says and
perpetuanas, although it was the manufacture of bays that was to
predominate in Colchester.

By the early seventeenth century their numbers had levelled off
to about 1,500, which represented a sizable proportion of the town's
population of about 10,000. Also by this time the immigrants had
been granted numerous privileges of trade, which amounted in
practice to having control over all the bays manufactured in the
town, including those made by the English clothiers. A rigorous
quality-control system was established at their Dutch Bay Hall (on

the site of the present Fire Office building in High Street) where the cloth was inspected and sealed at various stages of the manufacturing process. The first inspection took place after the cloth had been woven on the loom, and before any further work could continue, it had to be brought to the Raw Hall department of the Dutch Bay Hall where officers known as raw-hallers would inspect the cloth to ensure that it had been woven to the right exacting standards. The next inspection took place after the cloth had passed through the fulling and drying processes, from where it was taken to the White Hall department where the white-hallers would carry out a similar inspection process. At each stage of the quality-control procedure, if any cloth was found to be faulty in any way, then the offender would incur a fine known as a rawboot, the profits of which would be used to support the poor of the town.

Most of the finished bays found their way to markets of the Mediterranean, and the name 'Colchester bays' became something of a byword for quality. The early seventeenth century saw the town enter a new period of prosperity, with little unemployment and all the houses in the town occupied. This, of course, was largely due to the successful bay trade which had become the main industry of the town, providing employment for between a third and a half of all the town's occupied population. Of course, as might be expected, the success of the Dutch clothiers did incite some jealously among the English weavers, who on more than one occasion complained to higher authorities about the power of the Dutch clothiers, but successive monarchs continued to confirm the Flemings' rights and privileges as decreed during the reign of Elizabeth.

CHAPTER 6

Civil War and Plague

Unfortunately, the town's new found prosperity was to suffer something of a setback during the years of the Civil War in the 1640s, and particularly so during the Siege of Colchester in 1648. From the town's point of view this was indeed a cruel chance of fate, for until this point it had managed to escape any involvement in the fighting, despite having positioned itself squarely on the side of Parliament from the early days of the hostilities. But then, in the summer of 1648, the town was forced to play host to a large band of Royalist troops who were besieged in the town for eleven weeks by a Parliamentarian army.

The Siege of Colchester was the culmination of a series of events which had begun in Kent at the beginning of the year when, under the leadership of Lord George Goring, a large body of Royalist sympathisers had taken part in an uprising aimed at furthering the king's cause. Having crossed the Thames into Essex, the Royalist army, which by now had swelled to some 4,000 strong, set their sights upon Colchester where they arrived on 12 June 1648. The decision to target Colchester may have been based partly on the fact that one of their leaders, Sir Charles Lucas, was a resident of the town, and as such may have expected something in the way of a welcome from the townsfolk. However, if this was indeed the case, then they were severely mistaken, for if anything the people of Colchester felt nothing but mistrust for the Lucas family, who from the early years of the war had been staunch supporters of the king. Although the men of Colchester launched a limited attack on the advancing Royalist forces, they had little choice but to allow them entry into the town.

It is, of course, easy to be wise after the event, but had the people of Colchester made more of a stand and managed to hold out for just a further twenty-four hours, they would have been relieved by an equally large body of Parliamentarian troops which, led by Sir Thomas Fairfax, arrived on the outskirts of the town the following day. Fairfax's first reaction was to seek the immediate surrender of the Royalist forces in the town, thereby bringing the potential conflict to a swift end. Lord Goring, however, was in no mood to submit to Fairfax's demands and a fierce battle ensued in the vicinity of the

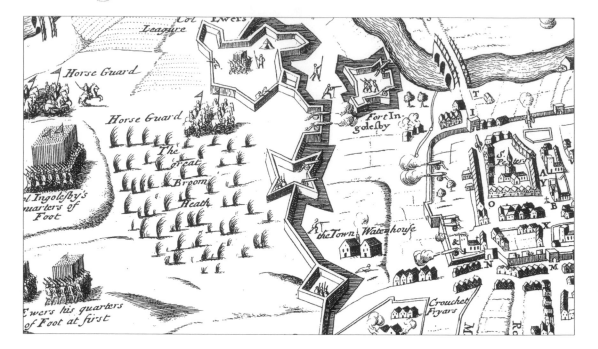

Head Gate as Fairfax's troops attempted to storm the town. The skirmish lasted for several hours and resulted in the death of several hundred men from both sides. At the end of the day, Fairfax decided that he was not prepared to risk the lives of any more of his men in such an action, and began to make plans to besiege the town with the objective of starving the Royalist defenders into surrender.

The resulting siege lasted for nearly three months, during which time the beleaguered townspeople, who, it must be remembered, had been unwilling participants in the whole affair, were forced to endure a period of extreme hardship. Houses were plundered and in some cases destroyed by fire, some of the women were raped and the menfolk beaten or murdered, and everyone had to endure the stress of trying to survive on very little food and other supplies. The shortages increased in severity as the siege moved into its final stages. Horses and domestic animals became such a normal part of a person's diet that, as the siege progressed into its final days, it was said that there was scarcely a cat or a dog left alive, with those that were commanding a high price on the black market. In fact, according to one contemporary account, half of the side of a small dog was selling on the streets of Colchester for 6s (perhaps £25 in today's money), and many of the poorer folk had been reduced to living on rats, mice and mutton fat candles.

In the early stages of the siege, despite the close presence of the Parliamentarian army, the defending Royalists had been able to make numerous excursions out of the town on its eastern side for

Detail from a map showing some of the siege defences in 1648. Note the gun emplacements along the western wall of the town.

Opposite: The tower of St Mary's at the Walls church, from where Royalist defenders held the enemy at bay with their high-rise cannon.

the purpose of rounding up flocks of sheep or cattle to supplement their restricted provisions. For several weeks, the Royalists had also occupied much of the Hythe and the area surrounding St John's Green, which included the former abbey gatehouse and the Lucas family mansion. However, as the siege progressed Fairfax was able to slowly tighten the noose around the town with a ring of forts and earthworks, thereby eventually cutting off access to these areas. The Royalists, for their part, had also been busy setting up a ring of defensive gun emplacements, particularly along the western side of the wall, where they established their principal fort in the church-yard of St Mary's at the Walls. From this lofty vantage point they found themselves in a good position to take pot shots at the Parliamentarian troops as they busied themselves constructing their forts and earthworks. In fact, Matthew Carter, a quartermaster general in the king's forces and an important eye witness to the whole sorry affair, noted in his diary that his comrades had even managed to raise a cannon to the top of the church tower from where a royalist sharpshooter, known as the one-eyed gunner, had proceeded to cause havoc amongst Fairfax's troops as they worked on that side of the town wall.

As the siege progressed, Fairfax managed to deploy a number of heavy cannon (some retrieved from the Tower of London) in strategic positions around the town, from where he was able to pound the Royalist positions to good effect. The one-eyed gunner at St Mary's tower was dislodged and Royalist positions on St John's Green and at the Hythe were also overcome. One of the most

The Royalists are routed from their gatehouse stronghold.

View from East Bay across the river towards East Street, from an eighteenth-century watercolour.

determined attempts by the Royalists to break free from the Parliamentarian stranglehold took place on the night of 5 July when a large Royalist force, comprising 200 cavalry and 500 foot soldiers, made a determined attack on the Parliamentarian front line which had been drawn up near East Bridge. Sir Charles Lucas is said to have led the attack in person, commanding the cavalry, while Sir George Lisle led the foot soldiers. The Royalists charged down East Hill and crossed the river where they engaged the enemy in battle (the Siege House in East Street still bears the scars of this skirmish). The Parliamentarians were forced to make a hasty retreat and were pursued by the Royalists for some distance before the Parliamentarians once again regained the upper hand and drove the Royalists back into the town. And although Royalist excursions into the countryside for food supplies continued for some time after this, the capture of the Hythe and St John's Green had effectively brought to an end any further determined forays out of the town by the besieged forces.

Finally, on 27 August, the Royalist commanders reluctantly agreed to terms of surrender. By this time the townsfolk were in a wretched state; over 700 horses had already been slaughtered to feed the besieged garrison. Even the thatch from the roofs of the houses had been stripped to provide food for the remaining horses, and the starving townsfolk had began to gather daily at Goring's headquarters begging for him to surrender. One contemporary account poignantly captures the scene as large crowds of people, particularly the women and children, became ever more desperate to see an end to their plight. 'This they did every evening, bringing women and children, who lay howling and crying on the ground for bread. The

soldiers beat off the men, but the women and children would not stir, bidding the officers kill them, saying they had rather be shot than starved.' At last, Goring relented and decided to open one of the gates to allow those who wanted to leave to do so. As several people of the town poured out from the gate they found themselves being fired upon by the Parliamentarian troops who were under strict orders not to allow anyone to leave. But when the townsfolk continued, the Parliamentarian Colonel Rainsborough ordered his men to strip some of the women. After four of the women had been so treated the group decided to retreat back into the town, only to find that the gate had been closed, trapping them in no man's land. And here they stood for some considerable time before the gate was finally reopened and they went back inside. The action taken by the Parliamentarians against these poor women and others, who were only trying to escape from their wretched condition, may seem rather harsh, but from Fairfax's point of view the longer that he could maintain the pressure on the enemy camp, the sooner they would be forced to surrender.

And surrender, of course, they finally did. With just one day's supply of food left the Royalist commanders sent representatives to Fairfax to arrange for a treaty. By this time, however, Fairfax was in

The Siege House in East Street still bears battle scars from the time of the siege.

no mood to be gracious in victory. He had previously offered the Royalists generous terms of surrender which had been refused and now he was only prepared to offer the general soldiers what he described as 'fair quarter' and the officers 'rendering to mercy', providing that all prisoners held by the Royalists were immediately released. The terms were later clarified to mean that the ordinary soldiers would not be ill treated and would escape with their lives and the clothes they stood in. The fate of the officers, however, could not be guaranteed and their future would be decided at the discretion of Parliament. The town itself was to be spared from plunder providing that it agreed to pay a fine of £14,000 (later reduced to £12,000 – and worth about £1 million in today's money). This was indeed a bitter blow to the town, whose citizens had from the outset been unwilling participants in the whole affair. As it turned out, the town made the Dutch community pay half of the fine, a disproportionate amount considering that they only accounted for about 10 per cent of the population. At a later stage when Fairfax agreed to set aside £2,000 to be used for the relief of the poor of the town, the Dutch (who were responsible for maintaining their own poor) only received £100.

On the morning of 28 August, the Parliamentarian troops entered the town and formally accepted the surrender of the remaining Royalist soldiers, who numbered more than 3,500. In the afternoon Fairfax and his senior officers also rode into the town and entered the Moot Hall, where they held a council of war to determine the fate of their captives. It was decided that four of the Royalist officers – Sir Charles Lucas, Sir George Lisle, Sir Bernard Gascoigne and Colonel Henry Farre – were to be executed without delay. At four o'clock that afternoon the Parliamentarian Colonel Ewers was despatched to the King's Head Assembly Room, where the Royalist officers had been instructed to congregate, in order to lead the condemned men back to the Moot Hall. However, when he arrived it was discovered that Colonel Farre had made good his escape, although Carter reported that he was later recaptured. The three remaining Royalist officers were brought before Fairfax and bluntly informed of their fate before being led away to the castle to prepare for their execution. Despite requests for their sentence to be delayed for a few hours to allow time for the condemned to settle their personal affairs, they were told to prepare for their imminent death.

At about seven o'clock the prisoners were led out to the north side of the castle to face their executioners. They were met by Colonels Ireton (Cromwell's son-in-law), Rainsborough and Whalley and three lines of musketeers. Having decided that Sir

Charles would be the first to die, he was brought forward to take his place in front of the firing squad. 'I have often faced death on the field,' he said, 'and now you shall see that I dare to die.' He then knelt to the ground and spent some minutes in prayer, after which he rose to his feet, opened his doublet and called out, 'See, I am ready for you; now rebels, do your worst.' With that the musketeers fired off a volley of shots and Lucas fell dead to the ground, having been hit four times. Next it was the turn of Sir George, who was led forward to the same spot. He immediately knelt down and kissed the body of his friend before he too was similarly despatched. Almost at the last minute, Sir Bernard Gascoigne was reprieved because it had been discovered that he was a gentleman of Florence. The council of war, having learnt of his situation from one of his guards, had apparently decided not to risk creating any adverse situations abroad and decided to set him free.

The execution of Lucas and Lisle outside the north wall of the castle.

With regard to the rest of the officers who had been spared the ordeal of execution, most were handed over to the various Parliamentarian regiments where they were given the opportunity to secure their release upon payment of a substantial ransom. Lords Loughborough, Capel and Goring, being peers of the realm, were

ordered to be transferred to Windsor Castle to await their trial by Parliament. Loughborough was held in prison (including a spell in the Tower of London) for six months before he was released upon payment of a large fine and allowed to return home to his estates. Capel was also held for some time in the Tower of London, but just two days before King Charles was executed at Whitehall on 30 January 1649, he made a daring escape from his prison cell in the Tower (one of the very few to do so). He was later recaptured and

The remaining buildings of St Botolph's Priory were badly damaged during the siege. This drawing shows the western front with its round window still intact.

St Botolphs Priory, Colchester. 1946.

The priory ruins as they appear today.

beheaded on 9 March 1649. This, of course, leaves Lord Goring, the leader of the Royalist army and one of the main instigators of the whole affair. After spending some time in captivity, he was brought before a tribunal where he was found guilty and sentenced to be executed. However, he appealed to Parliament and his life was saved by the casting vote of William Lenthall, the Speaker of the House of Commons. According to Matthew Carter's version of events, the reason why Lenthall had sided with Goring was because some years previously Goring had advanced him a large sum of money, at a time when he was in difficulties, and this was his way of repaying the debt.

And so ended the dramatic chain of events which had begun as something of an adventure several months earlier. And despite the loss of life and humiliations borne by the Royalist soldiers, the real losers in this whole sorry affair were the people of Colchester. Their town had been wrecked, trade had been brought to a virtual standstill and the crippling fine imposed by Parliament had only added to their burden. And yet within just a few short years the town was seen to be picking itself up and rebuilding some of the 200 or so houses which had been destroyed. John Evelyn, the diarist, provided the following view of the town as he saw it on 8 July 1656: 'To Colchester, a fair town, but now wretchedly demolished by the late siege, especially the suburbs, which were all burnt, but were then repairing.'

Before we depart from events concerning the Siege of Colchester, there is a footnote regarding the fate of Colonel Henry Farre, the fourth royalist officer condemned to death after the siege, who managed to effect his escape. Despite Carter's statement that he had been recaptured, he apparently managed to avoid the executioner's axe. At the time of the Restoration he was commissioned as a lieutenant at Languard Fort, Felixstowe, and was later appointed as its governor. Interestingly, his name also appears on a belated petition for war relief submitted to the Essex Quarter Sessions in 1678 by a labourer named Thomas Petchy from Blackmore in Essex. Although thirty years had elapsed since the event, Petchy had apparently sustained injuries whilst fighting for the Royalist cause at Colchester, and now (following the Restoration) like many of his former comrades was in a position to benefit financially from compensation for injuries received. In order for a person's claim to be considered, it was a requirement that each petition should be endorsed with various signatories, including that of their former regimental officer. In Petchy's case this was Henry Farre and the former Royalist prisoner's signature is clearly seen on the surviving document.

Despite earnest attempts by the townsfolk to repair the extensive damage caused during the siege and to restore the town's cloth industry to its former thriving levels, the seventeenth century was to bring further woe to the people of Colchester. At the time of the Great Plague in 1665-66, often described as The Great Plague of London, the disease raged with greater severity in North Essex, and particularly in Colchester, where nearly 5,000 people died – slightly more than the entire royalist army in Colchester at the time of the siege – over an eighteen-month period.

The number of people who died was also equivalent to about half of the town's population at the time; if repeated today, the death toll would be in the tens of thousands. This was truly a catastrophe of monumental proportions, and one from which the town would take well over a hundred years to recover.

By the autumn of 1665 regular collections were being made in all the local churches in order to relieve those who were suffering, but the monies collected were not enough to meet the demand, and additional funds (in the form of a local tax) had to be imposed upon all villages within a 5-mile radius of the town. As the disease raged on into the following spring, further help was forthcoming in the form of weekly collections in London churches for the relief of those suffering in Colchester. Even the diarist Samuel Peyps made

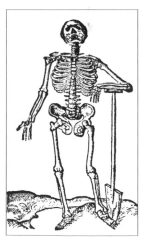

Nearly half of the population of Colchester died from plague in 1665-66.

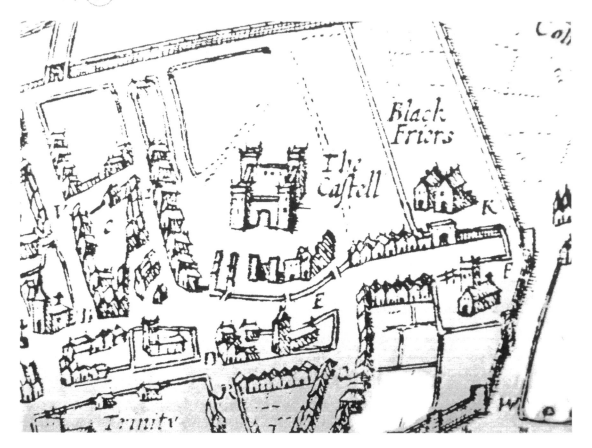

reference to the plight of the poor inhabitants of the town: 'July 4, 1666 – Thanks be to God, the plague is, as I hear, encreased [*sic*] but two this week; but in the country in general several places it rages mightily, and particularly in Colchester, where it hath long been, and is believed will quite depopulate the place.'

In order to try to contain the disease, two pest houses (hospitals for those suffering from the plague) were erected in St Mary's parish and at Mile End, where the sick could be housed and isolated, and other plague officials who were appointed to help contain of the disease could also reside. The buildings were apparently of timber construction, just one storey in height, and covered with a kind of tarpaulin or canvas. The surviving Borough Chamberlain's accounts for the period show that a sum of 7s was paid to Goodman Johnson for glazing the pest house in St Mary's parish, indicating that there must have been at least one window in the building. John Smith, the carpenter, was paid £25 in part payment for building the pest house at Mile End, and 10s 9d was paid for covering the same with tarpaulin.

Principal among the persons who were appointed as plague officials, and required to live alongside the plague victims in the pest

Detail from John Speed's 1610 map of Colchester, showing the castle and part of its defensive ditch and curtain wall.

houses, were those known as the 'Searchers of the Plague' and the 'Bearers'. Those appointed as Searchers of the Plague were required to search out and view the corpses of all who had died, and to report any cases of the plague to the constable of the parish concerned, and to the bearers who were appointed to bury them. They were to live apart from their families and, to the best of their ability, avoid contact with normal society. When they did venture out as part of the execution of their duties, they were to carry a white wand by which people might know them and so avoid their company. All those who were so appointed to carry out such duties were sworn in by the following oath:

> Yee, and either of you, shall swear that yee shall dilligently veiwe and search the Corps of all such persons as during theis infectious times shall dye within this towne, or the libertys thereof, or soe many of them as you shall or may have accesse unto, or have notice of; and shall, according to the best of your skil, determin of what disease every such dead corps came to its death, and shall ymediately give your judgement thereof to the Constables of the parish where such Corps shall be found, and to the Bearers appointed for the buriall of such infected Corps. You shall not make report of the cause of any ones death better or worse than the nature of the disease shall deserve. Yee shall live together where you shall be appointed, and not walke abroad more than necessity requires, and that onely in the execution of your office of Searchers. Yee shall decline, and absent yourselves from your familys, and allwaies avoide the societye of people, and in your walke shall keepe as far distant from Men as may be, allways carrying in your hands a white wand by which the people may know you, and shunn and avoide you. And yee shall well and truly doe all other belonging to the office of Serchers according to the best of your skill, wisdom, knowledg, and power, in all things dealing faithfully, honestly, unfeighnedly, and impartially. – Soe help you God.

And so, to all intents and purposes, those appointed as searchers of the plague were viewed as though they already had the disease. Those appointed as Bearers were required to swear a similar oath whereby they would promise to convey and bury the bodies of all plague victims, at night only. They too were to live apart from their families, to carry a white wand when venturing out into society and to remain ready at all times to carry out their duties as directed by the mayor of the town. For their troubles they were to be paid about 10s a week plus 2s for every body buried. The searchers, on the

other hand, received about 15s a week. Among other expenses incurred during the period of the visitation were payments made to the dog and cat killers (stray dogs and cats were thought to be carriers of the plague), and for various items of bedding and blankets for both the sick and the officials who resided in the pest houses.

The plight of the people of Colchester was also recorded by Ralph Josselin, the vicar of neighbouring Earls Colne, who maintained a personal diary throughout the period. Among the numerous references which he made concerning the situation at Colchester, the following entries are typical:

> Sept 16, 1665: God good in Colnes preservation, yet Colchester increaseth in illness being spread over the whole town.
>
> Oct 4, 1665: Wee remembered poore Colchester in our collection, neare 30s. and sent them formerly £4. God accept us and spare us for his mercy sake.
>
> Apr 1, 1666: Plague abates at London…, but it sadly increaseth at Colchester….

The High Street in 1638, on the occasion when Maria de Medici, the French Queen, passed through Colchester en route to London. Her daughter Henrietta Maria was married to King Charles I.

Although plague had been endemic in Britain throughout most of the Middle Ages, since running its course in the 1665-66 outbreak, the disease has never since posed major problems to the British Isles. Whether this is due to good management and hygienic practices, or just good fortune, nobody knows, and for a final word on the matter concerning the period under discussion, we will return once again to the pages of Ralph Josselin's diary: 'Nov 25, 1666. A very wett morning. The country cleare of the plague.'

CHAPTER 7

Decline and Recovery

According to the travel diaries of the late seventeenth-century writer, Celia Fiennes, Colchester appeared to be a well-appointed town with a thriving community. She arrived here in 1698 and was impressed by its appearance: 'The town looks like a thriveing place by the substantiall houses, well pitched [paved] streets which are broad enough for two Coaches to go a breast, besides a pitch'd walke on either side by the houses, secured by stumps of wood and is convenient for 3 to walke together.' She was also impressed by the number of people engaged in the production of cloth: 'The whole town is employ'd in spinning, weaving, washing, drying and dressing their Bayes, in which they seem very industrious.' She further noted that most of the houses were of timber-frame construction, with long roofs, great 'cantilevers' (jetties) and 'peakes' (gables), excepting those houses belonging to the Quakers which were of brick and in the London style.

Detail from an eighteenth-century prospect of Colchester showing the castle and tenter frames in the foreground. Note the length of cloth fixed to one of the tenter frames.

About twenty years later another traveller described the town in equally glowing terms. His name was Daniel Defoe, the author of *Robinson Crusoe* and *Moll Flanders*. He described Colchester as being an ancient corporation, well populated but still suffering from the effects of the Civil War. 'The town is large, very populous, the streets fair and beautiful, and though it may not be said to be finely built, yet there are abundance of very good and well built houses in it', he noted. He also visited the harbour area, which he described in equally complimentary terms: 'The Hithe is a long street, passing from west to east on the south side of town; at the west end of it there is a small intermission of the buildings, but not much, and towards the river it is very populous (it may be called the Wapping of Colchester); there is one church in that part of the town, a large quay by the river and a good Custom House.'

Both of the above descriptions paint a picture of a well-appointed town, well populated and fairly prosperous. But beneath this façade of well-being, there existed a very different image which may not have been immediately apparent to the casual observer. For despite the many fine buildings adorning the principal streets of the town and the apparently flourishing trade and industry, there existed an enormous gulf between rich and poor. Diseases such as smallpox were a constant scourge among the poorer classes and continued to claim lives at an alarming rate. In fact, during most of the eighteenth century the number of burials in the town continued to exceed baptisms.

The cloth trade in particular was going through a troublesome period. Continental wars and other problems affecting the markets in Spain and elsewhere had a severe impact on the overseas market for Colchester bays. Rightly or wrongly, the local clothiers had concentrated most of their entire production to satisfy the overseas markets, and particularly those of southern Europe. So in 1715, when the Spanish market became saturated, production of local cloth almost ground to a halt, sending thousands of people who depended on the trade for their income out of work and seeking poor relief. Hundreds of weavers left the town to set up elsewhere and many clothiers themselves also went bankrupt or decided to leave the industry altogether. The result was that in 1728 the Dutch Bay Company, which had dominated the production of bays in the town for nearly 150 years, was finally wound up, with the loss of many more jobs.

However, a number of individual clothiers continued to trade and produce bays from their own premises with a measure of success, but it was a bumpy ride and the decades that followed were blighted

An extract from the Dutch Bay Company's archives, dated 1727, showing the names of some of those chosen to serve as officers in the Dutch Bay Inspection Hall. The following year the Dutch Bay Company was wound up.

with problems. For example, in 1762 Isaac Boggis, a relatively suc-cessful baymaker in the town, came to the conclusion that if he was to survive in the industry, he would have to modernise and make use of the latest technology, even if that meant that some existing jobs would be put at risk. He had, in fact, planned to install a wool mill, a device used for cleaning and loosening the wool and which would have reduced his labour costs considerably, but he was warned in no uncertain terms against employing such a machine. In fact, the warning went so far as to say that his own family would be attacked if he were to employ such a device.

And it was in such an industrial climate that many clothiers decided that enough was enough and quit the business. Many others were forced into bankruptcy so that by the later years of the century the industry was in serious decline. The actual rate of decline can be fairly accurately gauged by an examination of surviving borough poll books, which record the voting of local freemen at parliamentary elections. For example, the records show that in 1768 there were 224 weavers listed, a figure which had reduced to just 39 in 1797.

Furthermore, estimates of the total number of weavers in the Colchester district in the early eighteenth century are placed at around 1,600, whereas by the end of the century the figure has fallen to about 200. The industry did, however, experience something of a mini-boom in the mid-1780s, at which time a French traveller to the town was able to report that the trade was flourishing with '500 looms clattering'. He also noted that the finished cloths were sent to London in four wagons that made the journey three times weekly, each carrying 250 pieces of cloth worth five guineas apiece.

But this upsurge in the trade was short lived and was to be followed by yet another period of depression from which the industry failed to recover. By the onset of the French Revolutionary wars in 1793, there were just four firms still making bays in the town. By the end of the hostilities in 1815 this number had been reduced to two, only one of which was able to limp on until the 1830s before finally calling it a day and selling up to a firm from Yorkshire. And thus an industry which had spanned a period of some 500 years finally came to an end.

There were, however, some positive aspects of town life in the eighteenth century. For despite the problems associated with the cloth industry, there were definite signs of an economic recovery in other areas from around the 1750s. A new emerging genteel class of society was also emerging which was to dominate local affairs throughout the decades that followed. The town was becoming fashionable, particularly as a result of the influence of families such as the Grays, the Rebows and the Weggs who, like many of their contemporaries, were building themselves new modern brick houses, in keeping with the fashion of the time.

Parts of the town were thus beginning to take on an elegant appearance, shining as a beacon, among the still large numbers of near derelict and dismal homes of the poor, which remained overcrowded and unsanitary for years to come. But for the richer classes this was an age of optimism and improvement. Social life came to be dominated by a succession of assembly balls and trips to the theatre, and in the main streets of the town a new breed of shopkeepers was emerging as an important part in the town's rapidly growing importance as a market centre. At the Hythe the situation was also improving. The number of commercial and industrial establishments increased by three times between 1760 and 1800. By the early nineteenth century these included eight granaries, nine coal yards, extensive maltings, salt works, a foundry, a lime kiln and a shipbuilding yard.

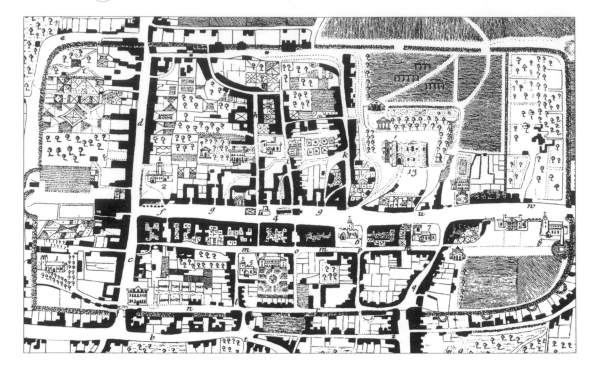

The population of the town was also at last beginning to rise (to 11,520 in 1801) and the growing volume of business and trade was being reflected in the establishment of at least two banks to serve the interests of gentry, farmers and other tradesmen. Advertisements in the press also paint a picture of respectability and progress, as demonstrated by the following example from the *Ipswich Journal* of July 1791: 'Colchester is a pleasant and healthy town; abounds in genteel company and has a market well supplied with fish.'

Colchester was at last beginning to recover from the depression of the earlier years of the century, and in the 1790s the economic trade of the town was further boosted by the establishment of a large permanent barracks at the beginning of the Napoleonic wars. This, in turn, was to lead to an upsurge of trade, particularly among the agricultural community whose produce, of course, was eagerly sought after. It was also, perhaps, rather fortunate as far as the town was concerned that war with France came at a time when the cloth trade was suffering so badly, and over the next twenty or so years the real effects of these troublesome times in the trade were partly cushioned by economic successes elsewhere.

The town had traditionally served as a mustering point for troops en route to the continent, and whilst stationed here they would be billeted in the various local inns – much to the annoyance of the local innkeepers. This is borne out in a report contained in the *Ipswich*

Plan of Colchester town centre, 1748. Note the relatively large areas of open space still available within the walled town area.

Journal of 21 November 1778: 'The burden of the soldiery in Essex is found insupportable, particularly in Colchester where the principal inns have 150 men each; a petition has been sent up to the war office praying relief.' In 1794, worried by the prospect of a long war with France, the town's innkeepers again petitioned the Corporation for proper barracks to be built to accommodate the growing number of troops arriving in the town. Their plea for action was rewarded later the same year when the first blocks of the new infantry barracks were erected on land to the south east of the town. By 1805, the barracks had been extended to accommodate up to 7,000 men and 400 horses.

Of course, once the town had been supplied with a permanent barracks, the various regiments that regularly visited the town would tend to stay that much longer, giving them the opportunity to get to know the area and its population better. This was particularly the case for the officers, who played a prominent part in the social life of the town.

As far as most people of the town were concerned, everyday life continued very much as normal during the war years, although the invasion scare of 1803 did result in a number of the town's inhabitants deciding to up sticks and leave for safer pastures. By the late

Detail from a map of Colchester in 1805 showing the position of the barrack blocks erected during the Napoleonic wars.

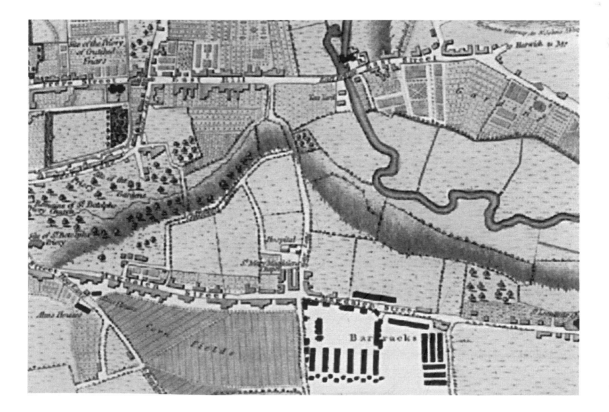

summer of 1803 the threat of invasion by Napoleon's army had become so serious that the garrison was put on orders to march at twenty minutes' notice. On 7 October a further warning of an imminent invasion was given by the commander of the garrison, urging the women and children of the town to leave at the earliest opportunity. The occasion is well described in a letter written by Mrs Taylor of West Stockwell Street to her daughter Ann, who was at the time living in London. (Ann Taylor and her sister Jane were to become famous for writing children's rhyme and verse, including the celebrated *Twinkle Twinkle Little Star*.) The letter was written on 11 October and included the following comments relating to the dire conditions in Colchester:

> On Friday last the principal inhabitants of Colchester waited on General Craig, the commander here, and received from him the most solemn and decisive warning of our danger and of the absolute necessity of the female part of the population, with their children, and what effects they can convey, leaving the town with all speed.... Heath is commanded to bake 25,000 loaves of six pounds each, every fourth day. Soldiery keep pouring in daily, the cavalry horses have not had their saddles off for several nights....The Rounds are going to Bath, lawyer Daniel is packing up his writings in sacks and with his family, will send them to Halstead. The East Hill people are flying thicker and faster.

The Taylor family themselves left for Lavenham in Suffolk shortly afterwards.

The expected invasion never materialised, but the large military presence brought some stability and prosperity to the town for as long as the war lasted and the garrison remained. At the end of the war, however, things began to change and within a relatively short period the number of troops deployed began to decline until they had vanished altogether. In fact, as far as the townsfolk were concerned, one of their last abiding memories of the former garrison may well have been catching sight of the soldiers returning to the town following the Battle of Waterloo. Apparently, one particular regiment, upon approaching the town, requested permission from their commanding officer to gather together some laurel shrubs from a garden which they were passing (the laurel being an emblem of victory) in order to decorate their colours. The officer in charge immediately halted the entire regiment to allow his men to pick as much as they wanted, and then with the regimental band playing, and with the words 'Waterloo' emblazoned in large gold letters

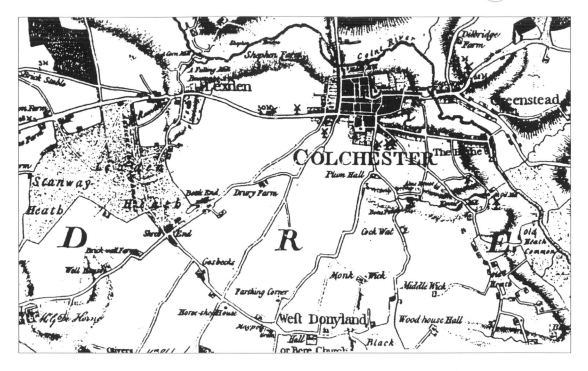

flying from their colours, they entered Colchester to the cheers of the large waiting crowd.

A period of bad trade followed the end of the war and within a few short years the barracks buildings themselves had been dismantled and sold off. This was indeed a blow for the town and the resulting unemployment among the poorer classes resulted in numerous bouts of rioting as they struggled to exist on extremely low wages and poor relief. And despite a few periods of respite, the resulting depression in agriculture which followed the end of the war was to last until after 1850 before finally giving way to a new phase of growth and prosperity.

Agricultural changes, mainly in the form of parliamentary enclosures, had been gathering momentum during the final quarter of the eighteenth century, although locally these were limited to the various tracts of heaths and commons which still surrounded the town. In particular, the 300 or so acres forming Lexden Heath and the smaller Old Heath Common had completely disappeared by the early 1820s.

Other changes affecting local agriculture at this time concerned the management of the Corporation's borough fields, or half-year lands (grazed from August to February), over which the burgesses of the town had exercised their grazing rights for centuries past (in the early nineteenth century these lands extended to over 1,000 acres).

Detail from a map published by Chapman and André in 1777, showing Stanway and Lexden heaths and Old Heath Common.

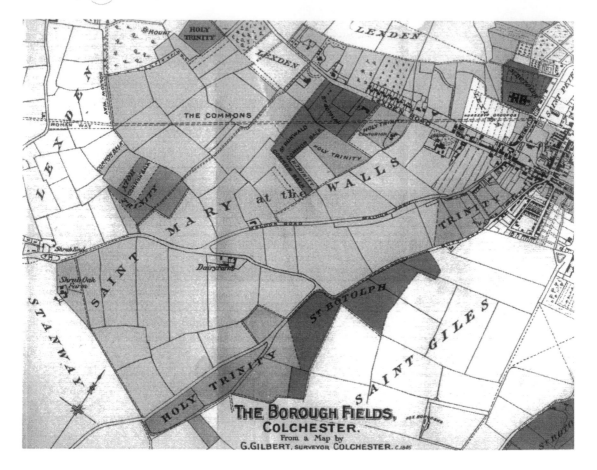

THE BOROUGH FIELDS,
COLCHESTER.
From a Map by
G. GILBERT, SURVEYOR COLCHESTER. c.1845

For most of the eighteenth century the Corporation had found itself heavily in debt and by 1803 this liability had risen to over £6,000. It must also be remembered, of course, that the free burgesses of the town were at this time still collectively liable for all debts incurred by the Corporation. And so in 1803 a decision was made to sell off the half-year lands, or to be more precise the rights of common over them, in a desperate attempt to offset some of their crippling debts.

No further action was taken by the Corporation until August 1807, at which time it was being threatened with high court action to recover some of the monies owing, which had by now increased to £7,249. They subsequently appointed a team of four conservators, from among the freemen, to survey and assess the lands in question with a view to accepting proposals from the various landowners to purchase the half-yearly rights of common over their lands. It had been decided to charge £30 an acre for meadow land and £20 an acre for arable. Obviously, as far as the landowners were concerned, being able to redeem these ancient rights of common over their lands with a one-off payment would enable them much greater

Map of the old Borough Fields over which the burgesses of the town exercised common grazing rights.

freedom of choice in their sowing and harvesting arrangements. As it currently stood, on Lammas Day (August 13) there was nothing to stop the burgesses of the town letting their cattle out to graze on the various plots of land, regardless of whether the landowners had finished harvesting their crops or not. However, the process proved to be a rather lengthy one with common rights over the affected lands still being sold off some twenty years later.

On the industrial front, despite the virtual collapse of the cloth trade and the slump in agriculture which had followed the end of the Napoleonic wars, there were signs of new beginnings and enterprise from a number of directions. Many of the town's former cloth workers had themselves found employment in the new silk industry which was already gathering momentum in a number of other former cloth-making communities, including Braintree, Bocking, Coggeshall and Halstead. The silk trade had been introduced to Colchester on a small scale in the 1790s, but within twenty years had grown substantially. In 1826 a large silk factory was built by Messrs Brown & Moy in St Peter's Street, providing work for some 400 women and girls, many of whom may previously have been employed as spinners in the bay trade.

Another enterprising venture which brought a measure of success to the town was the erection of a large malt distillery in Old Heath in 1812 by local businessmen Samuel Bawtree and George Savill. The new distillery was erected at a cost of £40,000 and was reckoned to be the largest of its kind in the country. By the mid-1820s the business had grown to such an extent that it was required to pay an annual levy to the government of £100,000, assessed at a rate of 2s per gallon of wort, or wash, produced.

Other smaller industries continued to develop and claim their share of the town's economic output. These included those engaged in the boot and shoe trade (which by 1800 was receiving nearly a third of all boys apprenticed under the requirements of the old poor law), brick-making, clock-making, tobacco pipe-making, various building trades and tailoring – which developed into one the town's major industries during the Victorian period, and which will be covered more fully in the following chapter.

As far as public utilities were concerned, the first quarter of the nineteenth century was to prove particularly fruitful. In 1808, engineer Ralph Dodd set up a waterworks company at the foot of Balkerne Hill, having it underwritten by an Act of Parliament. Two large reservoirs were constructed alongside a pumping station which housed a steam engine (the first in Colchester) to pump the water collected from the nearby springs to another reservoir located

A late Victorian view of Distillery Mill and pond, showing the location of Bawtree and Savill's malt distillery.

The Culver Street Distillery in the 1860s, when it was owned by Arthur Cobbold.

at the top of Balkerne Hill, close to where the present water tower building (Jumbo) stands. Unfortunately, when the steam engine was turned on at the official opening ceremony, the 700ft length of 'patent pipes' which had been laid up the length of Balkerne Hill were 'rent asunder like rotten paper'. And yet despite this unfortunate setback, the faulty pipes were replaced with others of cast iron and the scene was set for gradual improvement and expansion in the later years of the century.

In 1811, a body of men known as the Channel and Paving Commissioners was established by an Act of Parliament to carry out the measures of the Colchester Town Improvement Act. Those serving on the body were drawn from among the leading citizens of the town who, in the absence of any action by the Corporation itself, were to be responsible for such public services as street lighting, paving, the repair of roads and buildings and for improvements to the navigation of the River Colne between Colchester and

Wivenhoe, for which they had the powers to impose various taxes on goods arriving at the port.

One of the commissioners' first tasks was to provide public lighting for the main streets of the town. A series of oil lamps were thus installed around the town and in 1812 the contract for lighting and maintaining these lamps (nearly 500 in total) for the entire lighting season, which ran from September to March, was awarded to Samuel Bennell for the sum of £291 7s 6d.

In 1817 the first gas lighting apparatus in the town was installed in the rear of premises belonging to Messrs Harris and Firmin, who were chemists in the High Street. The initial experiment was limited to the lighting of their own shop and one or two neighbouring properties, although following the success of the scheme the commissioners granted them permission to lay pipes to a number of other nearby premises, and also requested that they lay pipes along the entire length of the High Street from St Nicholas' church to the top of North Hill. This work was duly completed and on 6 November 1819 the High Street was lit by gas for the first time. Over the next few years the supply pipe network was extended to several adjoining streets and by the mid-1820s most of the principal streets of the town were being illuminated by gas.

The Fire Office and Corn Exchange overlooking the market area in the High Street, c.1830.

This chapter closes with one of the most important events to affect the way in which many town governments, including that of Colchester, ran their affairs. The passing of the Municipal Corporations Act in 1835 brought in sweeping reforms affecting the way in which local governments were elected and how their corporate responsibilities were to be managed. Of particular concern to the existing Corporation of Colchester was that from henceforth all corporately held lands, and other property and possessions which had previously been owned by the free burgesses themselves, were now to be transferred to the Corporation in its own right. The new Act also brought to an end a number of ancient rights and privileges which had been bestowed upon the free burgesses of the town by successive monarchs since William the Conqueror. And so on 31 December 1835 the ancient Corporation of Colchester finally ceased to exist, being replaced by a fully elected council. Henceforth every council seat would have to be fully contested, and the first elected mayor under the new arrangement was none other than George Savill, who, it may be remembered, was the co-owner of a large distillery at Old Heath.

CHAPTER 8

Victorian Enterprise and Reform

By the middle of the nineteenth century, Colchester was developing industrially and emerging as an important centre for a number of new trades, especially engineering, boot and shoe manufacturing and ready-made tailoring. This was indeed an era in the town's history when it seemed as though an entrepreneurial spirit and perhaps a little bit of luck was all that was needed to succeed. There is not enough space available to do justice to the many local success stories which emerged during the Victorian period, but the following examples will hopefully serve to illustrate the importance of initiative in business and the knack of being able to turn opportunities into success stories.

One of the earliest entrepreneurs of the nineteenth century to have carved himself a place in the industrial history of the town was Hyam Hyam, the son of a Jewish immigrant, who must surely go down in history as one of the leading promoters of ready-made tailoring in Britain. Decades before the Montague Burtons of this world became leading lights in the production of men's ready-made clothing, Hyam Hyam was at the head of a tailoring empire which stretched the length and breadth of Britain – and which had as its power base the relatively unassuming town of Colchester.

The Hyam story begins in Ipswich, in Suffolk, where in the late eighteenth century Hyam and his father Simon were trading as pawnbrokers, jewellers and dealers in new and second-hand clothing. By 1803 Hyam had set up on his own account, first in Ipswich, then Harwich and finally in St Botolph's Street, Colchester, in 1817. Nothing much is known about his activities over the next few years, but by the late 1820s he was listed in a local directory as a 'Clothes Dealer', and was advertising for sale large quantities of ready-made clothing which he described as being 'home-made'. Whether this provides evidence of an early example of the integration of manufacturing and retailing, or whether the clothes were being made up by others elsewhere, is not known.

There is, however, some evidence that Hyam was providing regular work for several journeymen tailors in the town, who appear to have been sub-contracting some of this work to their female neighbours, who could be employed at cheap rates to complete

*Part of one of Hyam
Hyam's handbills offering
to the public a choice
stock of ready-made
clothing, c.1828.*

some of the finishing work, or other minor tasks. It would appear that Hyam was no fool and at some stage he must have decided to make a rather radical move, particularly as judged by the trading standards of the time. That move was to permanently sideline his force of journeymen tailors and to employ their female neighbours directly himself. All he needed to do was divide the manufacturing process into a number of individual tasks that each female worker could be trained to become proficient at, without needing the tailoring skills required to produce the complete garment. Thereby Hyam avoided the need to pay the higher wages demanded by the experienced tailors.

The experiment must have proved successful, for within just a few short years the Hyam family (by now several of his sons had joined the business) were being accused on a national scale of helping to put thousands of tailors out of work. In an article written in *Lloyds Weekly London Newspaper* of 12 November 1844, Hyam's name occurs alongside that of Moses and Son and other 'Flash Tailors' as being the among the principal retail 'slop' sellers in the metropolis (i.e. producing and selling cheap and nasty clothing at enormous profits) whose actions were being blamed for thousands of traditional tailors being forced out of work. In another report in

The Northern Star of 22 February 1844, Hyam is again being berated for taking advantage of hordes of 'white slaves' (female workers), who are prepared to eke out a miserable existence in doing slop work for the 'respectable' Messrs Hyam & Co. of Colchester, who it was said had up to 1,500 such workers on their books, and who probably were taking out work for as many more.

Although Hyam Hyam retired from the business in 1842, the expanding enterprise continued to grow under the direction of his sons who by 1845 were operating a string of retail establishments throughout the United Kingdom. It would further appear that the various individual branches of the business combined to form some kind of extended family federation where there existed strength in numbers, whilst retaining a degree of individual autonomy. Such an arrangement would also have ensured that although each branch of the business would have benefited from the combined strength of the family network, the failure of one part of the body would not necessarily bring the whole organisation crashing down. The Hyam family were therefore at the forefront of the tailoring industry nationally, and certainly would appear to have preceded that of Leeds, which began around 1853.

By the end of the nineteenth century a number of other tailoring firms had also established themselves in the town. Between them, they were providing employment for up to 5,000 female workers, either as directly employed factory hands or as out-workers in their own homes. The industry continued to thrive throughout the inter-war period, as mothers, daughters and granddaughters followed each other into the industry. However, from around the 1950s the industry entered into a period of decline, and within twenty or so years the trade had virtually ceased to exist. Today there is very little evidence to even suggest that a tailoring industry in the town ever existed. The former factory buildings have all but gone and the only sources of evidence which survive in plenty to bear witness to this once great local industry are those contained within the minds and memories of its former workforce.

About the same time that the Hyam family were enjoying some of their best years in the mid–1860s, another young Colchester entrepreneur was taking his first tentative steps into the world of business. His name was James Noah Paxman and at the age of thirty-three he was setting up his own engineering business in partnership with brothers Henry and Charles Davey. The new business was located in Culver Street, close to where the Culver Precinct now stands, and was known as the Standard Ironworks. The firm specialised in the

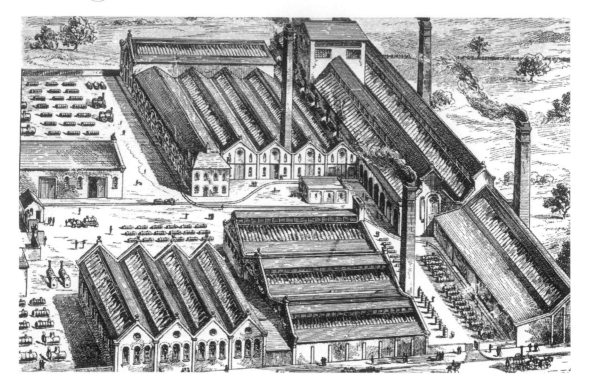

manufacture and repair of steam engines, boilers and agricultural
machinery. They were sharing their premises with another engineer
named Arthur G. Mumford, whose own firm (the Culver Street
Ironworks) was to achieve a good measure of success in the production of marine engines and donkey pumps, which were exported to
customers worldwide.

Part of Paxman's Hythe Hill factory in the 1890s.

The Standard Ironworks proved successful and in 1873 the firm
decided to move their operations to a larger site near the bottom of
Hythe Hill. The site chosen contained an old brick-making works,
which Paxman soon got back into production for making all the
bricks necessary for the new factory. By 1876 the factory was complete and the firm transferred its operations from its Culver Street
site, which was then taken over completely by Arthur Mumford. The
firm continued to specialise in the manufacture of steam engines
and boilers and was to pride itself on the fact that every component
needed in the manufacturing process could be made on the site.

Within a few short years Paxman's engines were being successfully shown at various exhibitions and receiving numerous awards
and medals, and later still were being used to provide the power to
light the exhibitions themselves, both at home and abroad. By the
early twentieth century the firm was producing an extensive range
of engines, each designed to meet the demands of the new breed of
high-speed generators. In 1904 engines supplied by the firm were

used to power the town's new tramway system and, also in that same year, the company produced its first internal combustion engine. By this time the company's workforce numbered about 600.

Many of the completed engines and boilers that daily left the factory were destined for such far-away places as South Africa, Russia, China and Japan. Transportation was usually by ship from the nearby River Colne and, more often than not, it was the first few hundred yards of the long journey (between the factory gates and the quayside) that proved the most difficult. Although not a great distance, as many as twelve heavy horses and, in later years, a large traction engine were needed to haul the heavily laden trucks along the bumpy road to the quayside.

In 1902 the company supplied and installed the steam generating equipment for the Mexico Gas and Electric Light Company in Monterey, which at the time was considered to be the most up-to-date power plant south of the Rio Grande. The Standard Ironworks had achieved both national and world acclaim and the scene was set for further expansion throughout the early twentieth century.

During the First World War the number of employees rose to over 1,800, including some 400 women, who along with the men worked in shifts around the clock. The production line was geared heavily towards secret war work for the government and included the manufacture of mine-sweeping equipment and parts for guns and depth charges. The firm also made 250,000 shells and large quantities of fuses and other firing mechanisms.

By this time James Paxman had retired from the business but he still made regular visits to the factory throughout the war years. One such visit was made on the occasion of the firm's fiftieth anniversary celebrations in 1915, when he toured the factory with two of his former workmen who had joined him at the beginning of the venture in 1865. James Paxman died at the age of ninety-one, bringing to an end an extraordinary career which also saw him rise to prominence in the field of local politics, when he served as Mayor of Colchester on two occasions.

In the 1920s, under the direction of James's son Edward, the firm continued to make progress and was soon turning its attention to the manufacture of diesel engines, for which the firm was to gain particular prominence. By the 1940s, they were producing engines for all classes of marine, rail traction and stationary work and during the Second World War supplied over 4,000 engines for use by the Admiralty to propel British landing craft in virtually every allied assault operation. All 'U' Class British submarines were also fitted out with Paxman's engines, making this the only time that both the design and construction of an engine for use by the Royal Navy had been entrusted to a commercial firm.

The firm continued to thrive during the post-war period and by the 1960s was easily the town's largest single employer, with a work-force of 2,500. But the good times were not to last and in recent years engine production has been moved to another part of the country and the workforce has dwindled to less than a hundred. It is perhaps a sign of the times, but the long-term future of this once major local employer is now looking decidedly bleak.

From the time of the Crimean War in the 1850s, yet another local industry achieved a certain measure of success. This was the town's boot and shoe trade which had been developing steadily over the previous decade, especially since the arrival of the railway in the 1840s which had enabled local traders to seek customers over a much wider area. The result was a sustained period of growth and expansion which was to see some of the more enterprising firms moving into larger premises and installing new factory machinery.

The new barracks, built during the Crimean War, also did much to bolster the trade, with thousands of local troops needing to be kept well shod. In fact, such was the growth of the industry over the next few decades that by the early 1890s the boot and shoe trade was poised to overtake engineering as the town's main business activity. Among the leading footwear firms at the time were Knopp & Son of Portland Road, who employed over a hundred men, A.C. George, who employed a similar number at his factory in Kendall Road, and numerous other smaller firms who employed up to fifty workers each. One such proprietor was William Warren, who operated a small factory employing between thirty-five and forty workers in premises near the old theatre in Queen Street. In general terms, very little information has survived as to how these factories operated or, indeed, any details concerning the conditions under which their staff were employed. But thanks to the recorded memories of one former worker at Warren's factory, we are able to gain an intriguing insight, albeit a limited one, into how things operated. The worker in ques-tion was Henry Watts, who started working at the factory in 1879 at the age of fourteen. Henry was later able to recall that even in a small factory such as this, numerous items of machinery had been installed to assist in the manufacturing process. These included a machine for sewing on the soles, a fore-part stitcher and a machine for closing the uppers. Hours of work at the factory were from 8 a.m. to 1 p.m. and 2 p.m. to 7 p.m., with everybody employed on a piece-work basis. Average weekly earnings were about £1 8s. Henry also recalled that

as a young apprentice he was able to 'bench' as many as seven pairs of men's hobnailed boots in a day.

The largest of the local footwear firms, however, was that belonging to an Irishman named John Kavanagh, who had begun trading in the town as a clothier and outfitter in Magdalen Street, before turning his attention to the repair and resale of discarded army boots. He was soon to be employing a workforce of nearly 400 after securing lucrative contracts with the military involving the annual repair of some 100,000 army boots. Added to this, his factory was producing an annual total of nearly 200,000 boots and shoes of every description. The prospects for expansion were thus looking good. However – and this is one of the great enigmas of the town's local industries – just when things were looking so positive, the industry entered into a period of steady decline. By the late 1890s the bubble had almost burst. Kavanagh's factory had closed down and within a few years many of his former competitors had followed suit. By 1914 the industry was virtually non-existent, and on the eve of the First World War a reporter in the *Essex County Standard* was able to refer to Colchester's boot and shoe trade as 'a thing of the past'.

The new barracks, built at the time of the Crimean War, was situated between Mersea and Military Roads and consisted of a range of single-storey timber-frame huts. The camp was first occupied by

Employees at Kavanagh's boot and shoe factory in the early 1890s.

infantry troops in January 1856 and in the same year a timber built church (today known as Camp Church), capable of holding 1,500 worshippers, was erected on the old Napoleonic military burial ground in Military Road.

The war with Russia had highlighted some serious deficiencies in the British army, not least the general lack of manpower available, but also the relatively poor health of many of the existing troops. To combat these deficiencies, at least in the short term, the government decided to raise a body of foreign nationals to fight under the British flag in the Crimea. The response from young men abroad was greater than expected and a number of units were established according to nationality, although made up largely of men of German, Swiss and Italian origin. One of the regiments formed was the King's German Legion, who were subsequently sent to the Crimea, but, as it turned out, arrived too late to fight as the war had come to an end.

This left the British government with a rather awkward problem – what to do with the newly formed regiments. Their own governments were not keen to take them back, particularly as they had enlisted to serve the interests of a foreign power, and subsequently several of the German regiments were ordered back to Colchester until it could be decided what was to be done with them. It was eventually decided to implement a scheme of voluntary emigration to the Cape of Good Hope in South Africa. Those volunteering had to be committed to remaining for at least seven years and be prepared to undertake various military duties on a certain number of days each year. The scheme was also designed mainly for married

The infantry barracks in 1865, showing the wooden huts erected during the Crimean War.

men and came with an offer of free passage for their wives and families and free rations for the first twelve months.

As most of the volunteers wished to go to the colony as married men there was apparently something of a stampede in the town as the would-be settlers strove to track down suitable brides to take with them. Most of them were successful and during a two-week period in October 1856, no less than 150 marriages were reported to have taken place in the town. Most of these marriages were solemnised at the Camp Church in Military Road, which at the time was not actually licensed to perform marriage ceremonies! However, that didn't stop hordes of young couples (sixty-four ceremonies on Sunday 19 October alone) meeting and completing their courtship in record time in order to qualify for the trip, some even being said to have struck up a last-minute marriage bargain at the church door. It was also said at the time that following some of the hastily arranged ceremonies, a few of the newly wedded couples were later unable to recognise their spouses at the crowded railway station, and several couples apparently got mixed up.

The Victorian period was also one of social reform, particularly in the areas of education and public health. In the early nineteenth century, facilities for education in Colchester were extremely limited. The few schools which did exist were mainly directed towards the better-off sections of the community and, with the exception of a

Camp church in Military Road. The church was erected in 1856 on the site of a former military burial ground from the time of the Napoleonic wars.

few Sunday schools, only the Bluecoat School (Anglican) in Culver Street and the Greencoat School (Non-Conformist) in Priory Street were providing any regular tuition for children of the working classes.

Things began to improve somewhat with the establishment of the Anglican-led 'National Schools Society' in 1811 and the Non-Conformist-led 'British and Foreign Schools Society' in 1814, which between them set about a programme of school-building throughout the country. Many of the schools built were small and cramped, and often consisted of just a single classroom where children of differing ages and abilities were taught together. But at least it was a start and a definite improvement on the earlier situation. Funding for the new schools was mainly by private subscription and charitable donations, as well as by small weekly payments made by the pupils themselves. At this stage, of course, there was no funding for education from central government, and even when the first grant was made available in 1833, the amount set aside was limited to just £20,000 for the entire country.

It must also be remembered that the majority of these early schools were established to provide an elementary education only, with the teaching based on the so-called monitorial system. Under this system, in theory at least, it was possible for just one master or mistress to teach a fairly large group of children – often a hundred or more – in a single classroom. This was achieved by the teacher directly tutoring a small group of the more able students in the class, who would then, in turn, relay the information to the other children in small groups.

And so from a couple of charity schools in the town at the beginning of the nineteenth century, by the 1840s there were at least a dozen others, all of which were being maintained by the various religious bodies, and providing an elementary education for a growing number of children. Things continued to progress and by the 1860s there was a school of some sort in every parish in the town.

But the situation was still far from satisfactory. Overcrowding was a serious problem, with as many as eighty or ninety children being crammed into the same classroom, while hundreds of others were unable to attend. The Education Act of 1870 did much to improve matters with the introduction of elected school boards whose primary objective was to ensure that enough school places were made available, even if that meant building new schools funded by the local rates. But this did not happen in Colchester – at least not for a while – and despite an official survey revealing a shortfall of at least 1,000 school places in the town, the local Anglican community,

East Ward School at the time of its opening in 1908.

East Ward School – class of 1908.

which at the time provided most of the voluntary schools, set out with some determination to rectify the matter. They managed to raise large sums of money both to upgrade existing buildings and to embark on a programme of new construction. Under the new Act the existing voluntary school societies had been given a short period of time to demonstrate that they could satisfy the demand for school places, or else a school board would be established. Whilst their efforts were only partly successful, they did manage to avoid the imposition of a school board for over twenty years.

By the early 1890s, however, it had become apparent that the ever-increasing financial burden of maintaining adequate school accommodation in the town was proving too much for the church authorities. In 1891 a survey had revealed a deficiency of 528 places, with a further 1,062 places below the required standard; in addition,

a further 450 places would soon be needed to cope with the expected growth in population. And with no money available to remedy the situation, a school board was finally elected to oversee the matter in 1892. One of the first items on the new board's agenda was to implement an immediate programme of expansion and improvement to existing premises. Such was the determination of the new ruling body that by the end of the century five new schools had been built: at North Street (1894), Old Heath (1894), Barrack Street (1895), St John's Green (1898) and Stockwell Street (1898). Between them they provided places for a further 3,000 pupils.

In 1902 the Balfour Education Act abolished the school boards and transferred their responsibilities to the local authorities. The old board schools now became known as council schools. Together with the older non-provided or voluntary schools which had previously been maintained by the Church and various other charitable organisations, they now received the bulk of their funding directly from the local rates.

In Colchester the new Act took effect from 1 April 1903, with the formation of a new Education Committee, chaired by Alderman Wilson Marriage. The new committee continued with the old board's programme of expansion, with further schools being built at

Old Heath School – class of 1904. The headmaster is Mr Alderton and the teacher Miss Wright. Note the good conduct and attendance medals being worn by several of the children.

Canterbury Road in 1903, Mile End in 1906 and East Ward in 1908. By this time the committee had authority over some twenty schools in the borough, which between them were providing tuition for over 6,000 pupils. By this time elementary education had become both compulsory and free for all children up to the age of twelve.

Another major issue facing Victorian Britain was public health. Once again the government had adopted something of a *laissez-faire* attitude towards the matter; it preferring to adopt a policy of non-interference and leave well alone, rather than accepting responsibility for the problems and enforcing remedial action. Of course the problems concerning public health were complicated: a lack of clean water, inadequate drainage and a complete ignorance of how diseases such as cholera and typhoid were transmitted were just some of the issues to be overcome. The main problem, however, was how to provide a constant supply of clean water, which was a prerequisite in the fight against epidemic disease and bad hygiene.

At the time of the 1848 Public Health Act, the town's water supply was being run by a private water company whose network of pipes only extended to some fifteen or so streets on the western side of town (about 600 houses). Even then, the company only supplied those householders who were willing to bear the cost of installing and maintaining their own service pipes and cisterns. A cistern for holding a reserve of several gallons of water was an essential requirement, for there was no guarantee of a permanent supply of running water. Indeed, the water company would often only commit to supply water on certain days of the week, and hardly ever on a Sunday.

The rest of the population had to resort to getting their water

A water-carrier and cart in Lexden Road, c.1890.

COLCHESTER WATER-WORKS COMPANY.

Whereas

Divers persons, who are Tenants to the Company, and pay an annual rent for receiving a supply of Water, are in the constant habit of conniving at, and allowing other persons, who are not Tenants, to

STEAL & CARRY AWAY WATER,

to the great injury of the Company, and in contravention of the Act of Parliament in that behalf made:

NOTICE IS HEREBY GIVEN,

That, with a view of putting an end to such practices, it is the intention of the Company to carry out to the fullest extent the provisions of the statute **48 Geo. 3., cap. 137,** *which imposes a*

PENALTY OF FIVE POUNDS,

as well upon the tenant who allows those who are not tenants to take the Water, as upon those who so take it: and any person or persons (except those guilty of the same offences, or either of them) who will give such evidence in either of the said cases, as will procure a conviction of the offenders, will be **REWARDED** *by the Company.*

BY ORDER OF THE DIRECTORS,

P. G. ABELL,

June 1857   MW Blount, *Agent to the Company.*

N.B. By the same Act, all persons who wilfully cause Water to run to Waste, are subject to the penalty of £5.

FENTON, PRINTER, 51, HIGH STREET, COLCHESTER.

A poster issued in 1857 warning against the stealing of water.

This view of 'Jumbo' from the 1890s shows the tower with its original heavy guttering.

from pumps, standpipes, wells, water carriers and, in a few cases, from local ponds and ditches. A report compiled for the town's Improvement Commissioners by the liberal public health reformer John Bawtree Harvey in 1858, revealed that over half of the main streets of the town were still not connected to the mains. The problem was particularly acute in the poorer districts of the town and which contained the greater number of people, who for the most part lived in crowded and cramped conditions. The report also showed that there were some 450 wells in the town, although most of them did not provide drinking water.

Even in situations where people did have access to a supply of clean water, whether from a local spring, a well or a pump, it would often be located at some distance from their homes, requiring a good deal of time to collect. Commenting on this matter in his report, Harvey made the following observation: 'In families where all who are able to work have to rise early and toil all day, it is a serious inconvenience and discomfort to them to have to fetch water at a distance from their homes on every occasion that it may be wanted, and oftentimes in rain, in cold, and in snow.' And yet despite the clear inadequacies of the prevailing situation, no real action was taken to address the problem for another twenty years. In fact, according to a report presented in 1873 concerning the sanitary condition of the town, one resident mentioned the fact that his washerwoman, who resided in the Old Heath district, had to cart every drop of water that she used more than a mile.

By this time, however, moves were finally afoot to address the matter. The Public Health Acts of 1872 and 1875 had been the catalyst for action. By the end of the decade the council had made arrangements to purchase the privately owned waterworks and to construct a large water tower (Jumbo) on land near to the top of Balkerne Hill. The construction of the tower, which at the time was the second highest building of its kind in England, was completed in 1883. And, with a holding capacity of 221,000 gallons, it provided a reliable source of water to the people of the town – or at least those residents who had access to the water supply network. Unfortunately, those living in the suburbs or the outlying districts would have to wait a number of years before they too would be able to benefit from the new system.

CHAPTER 9

The Great English Earthquake

Shortly before 9.20 a.m. on Tuesday 22 April 1884 the residents of Colchester were thrown into a state of panic and confusion when the town was struck by the shock of an earthquake. Not realising what had happened, people rushed out of their homes or places of work, convinced at first that the gas works at the Hythe had blown up, or that there had been an explosion at the barracks. And although there were no reported fatalities at the time (but this has since been found to be wrong), there was extensive damage to buildings over a wide area, particularly at roof level where it is estimated that about 10 per cent of all chimney pots were thrown down. The earthquake was the most serious to have occurred in Britain for over 300 years (the previous earthquake to have affected Colchester was in 1692) and thankfully has not been repeated since.

The epicentre of the quake was concentrated on the rural farming district a little to the south-east of Colchester, but it was felt over an area of some 53,000 square miles. It reached as far as Cheshire (180 miles away) in the north, the Isle of Wight in the south, Somerset to the west and Ostend in the east. The areas which suffered the greatest devastation, however, were those much closer to home, with the villages of Rowhedge, Wivenhoe, Abberton and Peldon being among the worst affected.

The local press capitalised on the public's interest in the quake, running stories and eye-witness accounts for several days afterwards. These included the following experience of the event given by Lord Alfred Paget, a well-known local and national figure, who at the time was on board his steam yacht which was moored at Wivenhoe. The yacht had only just returned from cruising in America and Lord Alfred had rowed out to the vessel to see how she had weathered the Atlantic crossing. He had no sooner climbed on board and glanced back to the quayside from which he had just left, when he heard a loud rumbling noise, and was then thrown from his feet as the shock waves of the quake surged across the river beneath his yacht. Lord Alfred later recalled what happened: 'Immediately the vessel began to shake and the people around me fell like ninepins', he said. 'I was flung against the rigging and, clutching on for dear life, wondered whether the boiler of the yacht had burst.' As Lord Alfred was

Earthquake 1884 Old Heath „Bell"

desperately trying to regain his footing, he looked towards the shore and witnessed the partial destruction of Wivenhoe. 'First the whole village seemed to rise up, the red slated roofs moving up and down as if they were the waves of the sea. Then, weaving crazily, chimney pots began to tumble over, crashing onto the roofs, showers of slates cascading down the sloping inclines of the houses either into the streets or through the huge gaps which appeared in the roofs themselves. The whole village appeared to be lifted up bodily.'

At North Station the stationmaster, Mr W. Blatch, was standing on the platform ready to start the 9.20 a.m. London Express. He recalled looking over in the direction of the town and thinking that his vision was blurred by a heat haze, as everything seemed to rise and sway, while a few seconds later he became aware of a rumbling noise: 'There was this rumbling noise at the same moment resembling distant thunder and directly the platform seemed to give a gentle heave, like the motion of a wave', he said. 'The passengers in the train all rushed alarmed to the windows of the carriages, and a number of men at work on the new asylum hurried down from the scaffold.'

In Lion Walk, in the centre of the town, part of the Gothic spire of the Congregational church came crashing down into the street below. This was witnessed by several local residents, including ten-year-old Herbert Johnson, who lived in the street, and was standing at the door of his house when the quake struck. 'Everything shook and bounced about', he said. 'And there was a great rumbling noise.

Damage caused to the Old Heath Bell Inn by the 1884 earthquake.

Then the spire of the church seemed to shake apart and came crashing down all over the place.' The event was also witnessed by Dr Alexander Wallace of Trinity House in nearby Culver Street, who stated that his house was shaken, the windows made to rattle, and the bells rung. He also recorded the fact that the shock wave from the quake appeared to be travelling in a north-easterly direction: 'The first thing we noticed was a rumbling, proceeding from the earth, not from above; a rolling sound indescribable, unlike anything else; coming from a distance in the south-west, passing under us, and proceeding in a north-east direction. The next thing we observed were falling chimneys all around, and the crumbling and fall of the spire of the Congregational Chapel close by.' Mr Wallace also added that the disturbance lasted for between five and ten seconds.

Nearly everybody who was living in Colchester or in the surrounding area would have been aware of the disaster and would have had their own unique story to tell. Laura Sibley, from Stisted, was working in Colchester as a domestic servant at the time. She recalled that there was a shelf on the wall of the house where she worked where all the jam pots were kept. When the earthquake struck all these pots began jumping up and down on the shelf. This particular memory was one that would stick with Laura for the rest of her life, and one that she would subsequently relate to her children and grandchildren. Another young lady who witnessed the event was walking in Sheep's Head Meadow, behind the castle, when to her astonishment she saw a cottage in Maidenburgh Street topple over

The Old Heath Bell and cottages opposite in the early 1930s.

Laura Sibley in her domestic servant's uniform, c.1890.

and become a partial wreck for no apparent reason – she herself had experienced no unusual sensation or ground movement whatsoever. Elsewhere, a young girl, whose grandparents kept a shop in East Stockwell Street, had decided to creep into the empty shop and help herself to some sugar without her grandmother knowing. She had apparently just opened the drawer where the sugar was kept and was about to help herself when the earthquake struck. The resulting commotion caused the bell on the shop door to ring which, in turn, brought her grandmother running into the shop half expecting to find that a customer had entered, only to find her small frightened granddaughter with her hands in the sugar drawer.

However, perhaps one of the most interesting accounts to have been recorded of that momentous occasion, particularly from a child's point of view, is that of Alfred Mason, who at the time was a five-year-old living in Old Heath:

It was a bright sunny morning, that Tuesday. I was sent by my mother down the hill to my father's market garden to collect some vegetables for lunch. It was a cauliflower she wanted, we were going to have it for lunch. There were not many people about then; the men were already at work and the women in their houses. I suppose I reached my father's place just a bit after nine. I told him what my mother wanted and he dug up a big cauliflower and gave it to me. He was too busy to talk to me so I set off back up the hill again. I hoped I might see someone to talk to, but there was still no one about. I was just in front of the Bell [public house] when I heard this tremendous rattling noise. The ground also began to shake beneath my feet. I thought I was going to be knocked over and the cauli-flower fell out of my hands. The noise was all around me and I was very frightened. I had no idea what it was. I just couldn't move and as I stood there I saw slates begin to rattle off the roofs of the houses on both sides of the road. Some of the chimneys were falling as well, and there were big cracks in the walls. It didn't last long, but the rat-tling sound was something I'll never forget. Our house had escaped with little damage – there were only some cracks in the walls and plaster off the ceilings. We could see that the roof of the Bell had caved in.

This page: *Culver shopping precinct – a hive of activity.*

Previous page: *The Town Hall.*

Opposite below: *Tymperleys Clock Museum, the former home of William Gilberd.*

Above: *Looking west along the High Street.
'Jumbo', the Victorian water tower, looms in the
background.*

Right: *Trinity Street, with Holy Trinity church and
the Town Hall.*

Above left: *Eld Lane – a popular shopping thoroughfare.*

Above right: *Police patrol in Sir Isaac's Walk.*

Left: *Red Lion Yard.*

Opposite above: *Jacks in St Nicholas Street, a popular hardware store.*

Opposite below: *The Maldon Road roundabout with the foundations of a Roman church in the foreground.*

Traditional shopping in Crouch Street.

Lakeside at the University of Essex.

Right: *The Rose and Crown Hotel,
East Street.*

Below: *A view along East Street
towards the town centre.*

Above: *Timber-framed buildings at the bottom of East Hill.*

Right: *A warm welcome awaits you at the Visitor Information Centre.*

Right: *Hollytrees Museum, High Street – once described as the best eighteenth-century house in Colchester.*

Below: *The Minories Art Gallery from Castle Park.*

Right: *Castle Park in springtime.*

Below: *Rear view of the castle.*

Opposite: *The castle and flower gardens.*

Castle Park: the fish pond (above) *and the boating lake* (below).

Castle Park: a place to relax (above) *and a venue for county cricket* (below).

Above: *Riverside cottages near North Bridge.*

Left: *Colourful houses in the Dutch Quarter.*

Opposite above: *Distillery Pond with Maitlands House in the background.*

Opposite below: *Bourne Mill and pond.*

Hythe Quay – once the industrial heart of Colchester, but now virtually inactive.

Modern housing has replaced industrial buildings at the Hythe.

CHAPTER 10

The Twentieth Century

Edwardian Colchester

At precisely midday on Saturday 26 January 1901, the mayor of Colchester, Claude Egerton Green, read out an important announcement to a large crowd which had gathered at the town's Head Gate. The mayor's message was to proclaim the accession to the throne of Queen Victoria's son Edward, following her death just a few days earlier. The announcement itself was brief and to the point, and followed closely the official format provided by central government, but in Colchester they decided to milk the occasion for all it was worth. Not content with a single reading of the proclamation, they decided to repeat it three times in quick succession. In fact, it was something of a local tradition that important announcements were made at three of the town's historic sites, and the mayor obviously decided that this event was to be one of those occasions. The second reading took place on the steps of the mayor's residence (East Hill House) not far from the site of the old East Gate at top of East Hill, with the third reading taking place at the site of the old Obelisk in the High Street (near the Red Lion hotel). Finally, the gathering converged on the steps of the Albert School of Art and Science (now the Co-op bank) where they joined together in singing the National Anthem, and in this manner the people of Colchester were ushered into the Edwardian Age.

The following year there was further reason for celebration with the opening of the new Town Hall. The building is still regarded as the most striking structure in the High Street, dominating the town centre and being a near perfect example of the revived Renaissance of the late Victorian period. It was opened by the Earl of Rosebery (a former Prime Minister) on 15 May 1902 and is the third in a line of municipal buildings to have occupied this same small plot of land since Norman times.

Following the decision to demolish its predecessor in 1897, competitive designs for the new building were sought from a number of eminent architects. Norman Shaw, one of the greatest architects of the time, was asked to adjudicate. From a total of eight entries submitted, Mr Shaw awarded first place to Mr John Belcher of London.

Mr Belcher's design was grand, impressive and flamboyant and was to become something of a role model for the building of neo-Baroque town halls during the Edwardian period. It also won acclaim from the architectural critics of the day, including the following from *The Builder* magazine: 'Mr Belcher shows a fine, stately-looking plan which combines dignity with efficiency.'

The architect's original estimate to complete the structure was in the region of £36,000, excluding many of the planned external and internal embellishments. In fact, the final cost of construction, which was awarded to the firm of Kerridge and Shaw of Cambridge, came to about £55,000, of which about £12,000 was raised by local benefactors. From the outset the council had adopted the principle that whilst such parts of the building as were necessary for the administration of the town, and for the use of the inhabitants at large, should be erected at public cost, the embellishment of the building, including pictures, statues and stained glass etc., should be funded privately. The largest single gift was made by the mayor for 1897-98, James Paxman, who generously offered to defray the entire cost of the clock tower, which was estimated at about £3,000.

The foundation stone for the new building was laid by HRH the Duke of Cambridge (first cousin of Queen Victoria) on 31 October 1898. The giant stone, weighing two tons, was supplied by L.J. Watts

The mayor of Colchester, Claude Egerton Green, proclaims the accession to the throne of Edward VII in 1901. The people have gathered at the site of the old obelisk in the High Street, near to the Red Lion Hotel.

Ltd of Colchester, and had a small hole (12in by 9in) cut into the top into which was placed a parchment record signed by the mayor, the Duke of Cambridge and the town clerk, as well as a copy of the official programme of the day's proceedings. The type of stone used is known as Brown Portland, and is similar to that used for the construction of St Paul's Cathedral. One important announcement made at the time was to the effect that Her Majesty the Queen had given her permission for the tower of the building to be named the 'Victoria Tower', following a request made by James Paxman.

Building work began on 2 January 1899 and took just over three years to complete. It had been decided to place a statue of St Helena, the town's patron saint, on top of the tower and the job of obtaining such a monument was given to Councillor Arthur Jarmin. In pursuit of this quest he apparently travelled as far afield as Italy, but being unable to find a statue of St Helena, and perhaps feeling a little desperate, he finally settled for a statue of the Virgin Mary

An engraving of 'The Pieman' and the High Street Obelisk from 1792.

Mr Belcher's award-winning design for the new Town Hall.

which he duly had shipped back home. The statue was placed on top of the tower from where it still surveys the surrounding countryside, whilst gazing in the direction of Jerusalem.

Below the statue, set at the four corners of the tower, were placed four large bronze ravens, which are symbolic of the Port of Colchester. Just a few years ago one of these ravens actually fell from its lofty perch and landed in the High Street, narrowly missing a passer-by. In order to repair the damaged bird, one of the other ravens had to be temporarily removed to act as a pattern, leaving just two ravens on top of the tower for a period during 1994.

The new Town Hall at the time of its opening in 1902. Note also the approaching steam lorry and line of horse-cabs waiting at the nearby cab rank.

Today the Town Hall remains a working building at the centre of local life and civic affairs. It houses the mayor's office, council chambers and magistrates' courts, as well as the great Moot Hall where grand civic events such as the annual oyster feast are held.

Another new building which was erected in the High Street in the 1900s was the Grand, one of a new breed of variety theatre, which was later to be renamed the Hippodrome. The Edwardian era was the age of vaudeville, with music halls and theatres throughout the country regularly playing to packed audiences.

The High Street with the Hippodrome theatre on the left, c.1912.

Before the building of the Grand, the principal place of entertainment in Colchester was the Theatre Royal in Queen Street, which had been built in 1812 a cost of £3,000. The building had seating for 1,200 persons, with admission charges ranging from 6d for a seat up in the high gallery to 3s 6d in the front stalls. By the late Victorian period, however, the building had become rather run down and a decision was taken to repair and refurbish it. This began in 1901 and included the installation of electric lighting, warm air heating and a new range of seating. And, of course, the improvements could not have come at a better time, as the building was shortly to experience some serious competition from the new theatre being built in the High Street.

The new High Street building was almost twice the size of the Theatre Royal, with seating for around 1,700 on three levels. It opened to the public on Easter Monday 1905, when a packed house was entertained with a play entitled *The Walls of Jericho*. After a few weeks, however, the programme on offer was of a very different nature, being one of variety and entertainment all the way. Audiences were treated to acts involving educated bears, performing monkeys and even elephants, for which the stage had to be specially reinforced! Performances were repeated three times daily – a matinée performance in the afternoon and two more in the evening, with admission charges starting at just 3d for a seat in the gallery. Sidney Murrells, who was born in 1892, had fond memories of his visits to the Hippodrome:

> We used to go there every Saturday night, and we always had to queue. We paid threepence for a seat in the gallery, or if you took a young girl with you, you had to pay sixpence to go in the pits. I remember seeing Jack Johnson the boxer and Marie Lloyd the singer and whenever they used to sing a song we would all join in with the chorus. We had a lovely time; a penny packet of Woodbines and a ha'penny box of matches, we were set for the week.

It was also around this time that 'moving pictures' began to appear as part of variety programmes. The short clips of flickering film were usually slotted in at the end of the performances and were shown on an early type of film projector known as a bioscope. The pictures would be projected onto a screen using a 6,000 candle-power lamp and would have included such subjects as the Paris Exhibition, cavalry exercises at Aldershot and the Boer War.

In November 1910 both the Hippodrome and the Theatre Royal found themselves with a new rival in the form of the town's first cinema, which opened in St John's Street, and which was called the Electric Theatre (later the Cameo). The new cinema was soon screening pictures continuously from 2.30 to 11 p.m., with the musical accompaniment provided by a piano or gramophone. In later years, this was also the first cinema in the town to screen 'talking pictures'. The following year the Vaudeville Electric Theatre (later the Empire) opened in Mersea Road, and was the first picture house in the town specifically constructed as a cinema. The new building had seating for around 600 and, in the first six weeks after opening, over 34,000 people had attended, averaging over 700 a day. In 1920 the Hippodrome theatre also became a cinema and, by the 1930s, these three houses had been joined by the Playhouse and the Regal, making five picture houses in the town all showing the latest films. The old Theatre Royal was destroyed by fire in 1918.

The Edwardian era was also the age of the travelling showman – flamboyant entertainers who toured the country staging their own brand of live variety. And they didn't come much bigger than Buffalo Bill and his famous Wild West Show. After arriving in Britain in the spring of 1903 and staging an initial performance at

The opening night's programme at the new Grand Theatre on Easter Monday 1905.

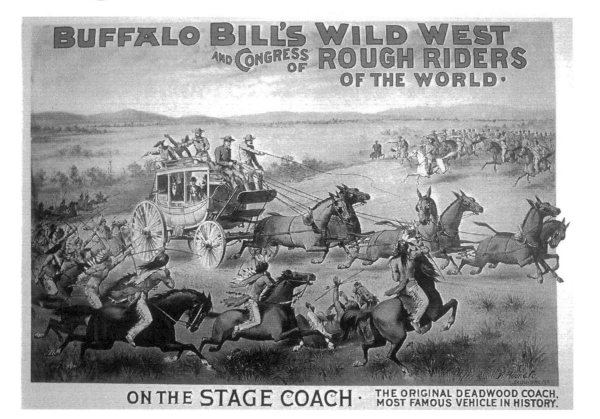

BUFFALO BILL'S WILD WEST
AND CONGRESS OF **ROUGH RIDERS**
OF THE WORLD.

ON THE STAGE COACH · THE ORIGINAL DEADWOOD COACH, MOST FAMOUS VEHICLE IN HISTORY.

Olympia, the show embarked upon a nationwide tour, calling at towns and cities throughout the country, including Colchester. The show arrived in the town in the early hours of Friday 4 September on three specially hired trains from their previous engagement at Southend. Crowds of people had risen early to welcome the visitors to the town as their large entourage, which included hundreds of Sioux Indians, Plains cowboys, Russian Cossacks and Mexican vaqueros, all mounted on beautiful horses, made their way to the showground at Reed Hall. Within a few hours a large temporary camp had mushroomed out of nowhere to house and feed the workers and performers, and by midday a spacious arena measuring 400ft by 210ft had been erected with undercover seating for 10,000 spectators.

In the afternoon the town almost came to a standstill as crowds flocked to see the show. Many schools were forced to give a half-day holiday because of widespread absenteeism, and several shops and businesses closed early to enable their staff to attend. The event began like a whirlwind as over 300 riders galloped into the arena at breakneck speed, before swerving to a halt in lines abreast. Colonel 'Buffalo Bill' Cody rode to their head, swept off his sombrero and proclaimed, 'Ladies and gentlemen, permit me to introduce to your

The arrival of Buffalo Bill's Wild West Show in the town caused much excitement.

notice the Congress of the Rough Riders of the World.' The performance then began and was a success from start to finish, as acrobats,
jugglers, cowboys, Indians and Cossacks thrilled the crowds as they
went through their various routines. Buffalo Bill himself also put on
a fine display of marksmanship whilst riding a galloping horse and,
for the grand finale, the audience was treated to what had been
billed as the greatest of living dramas – *The Attack on the Deadwood
Stage*.

The entire production was repeated in the evening with the arena
illuminated by electricity. And despite having to endure appalling
weather, in the form of a severe thunderstorm, over 8,000 were in
attendance. At the end of the show the clearing up process was carried out with the same order and professionalism that just a few
hours earlier had seen it all put together. By midnight the entire
camp had been dismantled, the equipment loaded on to the waiting
trains, and the show was on its way to its next venue.

Perhaps the premier social event of the Edwardian period, however,
was the staging of the Great Colchester Pageant in June 1909. This
was when more than 3,000 local people, including hundreds of
schoolchildren, donned costumes and re-enacted the town's history
from the coming of the Romans to the close of the Civil War. The
event, which took nearly two years to plan and organise, was staged
in the grounds of the Lower Castle Park during the week of 21-26
June.

The art of pageant-making had become quite popular, with successful events having already taken place at Sherbourne (1905),
Warwick (1906), Bury St Edmunds (1907) and Dover (1908). The
man responsible for the success of these events had been Britain's
'Pageant master' himself, Louis Napoleon Parker, who had also
agreed to take on the Colchester project. A committee was formed,
subscription and guarantee lists drawn up, and a start made on writing the script, designing the scenery and making the costumes. At
one stage a public meeting was held in the Moot Hall at which Mr
Parker was guest speaker. He began by explaining exactly what a
pageant was and then gave everyone present an idea of what to
expect by reading aloud sections from the prepared script.

In the final weeks leading up to the big event 'Pageant fever' well
and truly gripped the town. Many of the main streets had begun to
take on a carnival appearance, with several buildings displaying
pageant banners, flags and brightly coloured bunting. To help those
planning to visit the event from outside the area, the Great Eastern
Railway laid on several special trains, with reduced rates for those in

possession of a pageant ticket. Advance ticket sales had realised over £6,000 and it was evident that the event would be at least a financial success. The large grandstand, which had previously been used at Dover, could accommodate upwards of 5,000 people, all seated under cover.

A scene from the Colchester Pageant of 1909 with the Roman Temple of Claudius in the background.

On the great day itself bright sunshine and a large enthusiastic crowd were on hand to welcome the mayor of Colchester, W. Gurney Benham, and his party of distinguished guests to the pageant arena as they assembled for the official opening. The event was opened by the Lord Mayor of London, Sir G. Wyatt Truscott, who offered his congratulations to the town for both having initiated the idea of staging a pageant in the first place, and secondly for having secured the services of Mr Parker, whose name alone, he said, was enough to ensure success. At the end of the opening address Mr Parker called upon the heralds to announce the pageant open.

The three-hour-long spectacle which followed was greeted with cheering and applause from the large crowd, who clearly appreciated the enthusiastic and professional approach displayed by the large team of amateur performers. Every small detail of known history had been skilfully woven into the text, resulting in a fast moving spectacle of incident and colour from start to finish. On the final day of the pageant the proceedings were extended to include a special tribute to Mr Parker, who was subsequently conveyed around the arena in a Roman chariot to the sound of loud cheering, from performers and audience alike.

And so came to an end a week of festivity and merriment where a combined audience of nearly 60,000 had been entertained. Despite the miserable weather which descended on most days' proceedings, the event was nevertheless able to show a profit of £700. On Friday 2 and Saturday 3 July, a special auction of material and property used in the pageant was held at the premises of auctioneer Herbert Baskett on North Hill. Among the items offered for sale was the Roman Temple of Claudius, Boudica's chariot and countless pieces of armour and weaponry. The sale realised approximately £250 with muskets selling for a 1s a piece, Roman spears 6d, swords and daggers 4s 6d a bundle and with Boudica's chariot fetching seven and a half guineas (£7 17s 6d).

The Edwardian years must also be remembered for the dramatic changes which took place in transport. In 1901 the roadways of England were still very much dominated by the horse. Almost every kind of wheeled vehicle was horse-drawn and nationwide the number of horses so employed ran into the millions. In Colchester all of the 115 licensed hackney carriages (the highest number ever) were horse-drawn, as were all other types of cart, wagon and omnibus which filled the streets of the town.

The exceptions were confined to just a handful of motor cars which were slowly arriving in the town. The first motor vehicle in the town was owned by Arthur Stopes, manager of the Colchester Brewing Company on East Hill, who had taken possession of a Daimler Wagonette in 1896. The sight of this car chugging its way up and down East Hill must have caused quite a stir at the time, for it would probably have been the first time that the majority of townspeople would have seen one. The second car in the town was a Panhard owned by Arthur Berry, who was one the town's early omnibus proprietors. Both cars featured the early type of tiller steering and in appearance were little more than horse carriages which had been fitted with an engine. And despite the engineering problems encountered by early motorists, and the fact that all fuel had to be collected from the quayside at the Hythe, the seeds had been sown for what was to become one of the popular inventions of modern times.

Whilst ownership of a car may have been reserved for the privileged few in the early years of the century, yet another form of transport was shortly to be introduced to the Edwardian public. This was the town's new electric tramway system, which was opened on 28 July 1904. For the first time, an affordable and convenient means of transport had been made available for the masses and, for just one penny, one could travel from the centre of town to either North

The cover of the catalogue for the pageant auction, at which items used in the display were to be disposed of.

Station, Lexden, Harwich Road or the Hythe. The trams, which were all open-top double-deckers, began their daily service before 6 a.m. and continued until 11.30 p.m.

The opening ceremony was performed by the mayoress, Mrs Gertrude Barritt, who took pleasure in powering up the first tramcar to the applause and cheers of the large assembled crowd. She then helped to drive the tram on its maiden journey to Lexden. The occasion was a success and, despite the wet and miserable weather, the people of Colchester turned out in their thousands to experience their first tram ride. By the end of the day the trams had carried more than 10,000 passengers, collecting over £42 in fares. Also present at the opening earlier in the day had been the local photographer, William Gill, who within just one hour of the official opening was offering souvenir picture postcards of the event for sale to the public.

Conductors and motormen (drivers) on the tramway had a working week of sixty hours, with wages ranging from 18s to 22s a week. Discipline was strictly maintained and those committing a serious offence, such as speeding or failing to halt at a compulsory stop, faced immediate suspension or even dismissal. Harry Salmon (born 1895) served as both a conductor and driver on the Colchester trams in the years leading up to the First World War, and at the age of ninety-five recalled some of the conditions that he and the other drivers had to put up with all those years ago:

A tramcar at the bottom of Hythe Hill. The presence of a female conductor dates the picture to sometime during the First World War.

Rules were very strict you know. You dare not miss a passenger if he was up the road somewhere, or you'd be for it. I can remember one day, when working as a conductor, being called into the office by the Chief Clerk, who asked me if I would be interested in learning how to become a driver and, of course, I jumped at the chance. Anyway, I had my time of instruction on the road under the supervision of a motorman, and then I went into the sheds for a certain amount of time learning about the workings of a tram, before finally having to complete an oral examination before the General Manager. I can clearly remember that he asked me twelve questions and on the last question he said to me, 'You are going along Lexden Road with your tram at 2½ miles an hour and if a little child ran right across in front of your tram, what would you do?' 'Reverse and give the car power, Sir', I said. 'Have you not been taught never to use your magnetic brake like that?' he said to me. 'But you told me that I was only travelling at 2½ miles an hour and at that speed the motors wouldn't generate enough electricity to work the brakes', I said. 'Stop, get out of my office and don't think you know everything,' he said and with that I became a driver.

Despite the obvious convenience of the trams, the network itself was extremely limited and, with increasing competition from outside motor bus companies particularly during the 1920s, it was finally decided in 1929 to abandon the service altogether in favour of a fleet of new motor buses.

Colchester at War

In the months following the declaration of war on Germany in August 1914, Colchester was transformed into a giant military camp as thousands of troops bound for the continent poured into the town. Temporary camps were set up on every available open space, including Abbey Field, Middlewick, Wivenhoe Park and the Recreation Ground, and as even more troops arrived in the town they were billeted in the homes of ordinary people. One person able to recall these events was Jack Ashton (born 1902) who could remember the town being flooded with soldiers:

I can remember Kitchener's army coming up. They all came in their civvy clothes, just as they were called up. They put them on the Abbey Field and us kids used to go up there on Sunday afternoons and watch them play 'housey housey' (bingo). Butt Road was

Soldiers parading on the Abbey Field in the early twentieth century. Note the tented encampment in the background.

flooded with them coming into the town – that was when the tradesmen of Colchester did the best trade of their life. Eventually they came round to all the householders for them to take two or three soldiers, and you had to have a very good case not to take them in because they would put four in a front room, sleeping on the floor.

Albert Bridges (born 1908) also recalled that most people at the time had to provide accommodation for soldiers: 'Nearly everyone had a soldier or two billeted with them, no matter how many children they had. We had two soldiers staying with us and they had to sleep on the floor.' And the billeting of soldiers was not confined to any particular social group, although it would appear that those responsible for organising the accommodation did at least try to match people from similar backgrounds. Elizabeth Compton (born 1902), whose family lived in a large eight-bedroom house in Inglis Road, also had to do their bit to help: 'We had about two married couples staying with us – officers and their wives. At first they had their meals with the family, although later my mother gave them the dining room while we had the study and drawing room.'

For the first few months of the war the people of Colchester had very little direct contact with what was happening abroad, apart from seeing trainloads of wounded soldiers returning home from the front. Jack Ashton recalled that they used to stand and cheer the wounded soldiers coming into St Botolph's station, and Winifred Fairhead (born 1898) remembered seeing the ambulances going to and fro past their North Station Road home virtually all the time. Lilian Oakley (born 1908), who attended St Mary's Church School in Balkerne Lane, had a particular reason for wanting to watch the

Part of Kitchener's Army in Colchester during the early years of the First World War.

wounded soldiers passing by her schoolroom on the way to the hospital:

> I can remember our teacher asking us children to bring to school any old scraps of material that our mothers could spare, including pieces of old woollens and dresses etc., which we then had to painstakingly pull to pieces, thread by thread, until we had collected enough fibre to provide the stuffing for several pillows. When they were finished they were covered with a red and yellow sateen material and were used as head rests by the wounded soldiers returning from the war. And I can remember standing with the others on top of a line of wooden forms, peering out of the classroom windows into Balkerne Lane, as a procession of open-top cars carrying the wounded soldiers passed by on their way to the hospital.

Early in 1915, Colchester was attacked by a military force for the first time since the siege of 1648. The airborne attack, which was one of the earliest of the war, happened on Sunday 21 February at about 8.40 p.m., when the streets were still full of soldiers and people returning home from the various places of worship. The pilot of a single German aircraft, which had been observed circling the area for the previous forty-five minutes, dropped a bomb which landed in the rear garden of a house in Butt Road. Thankfully nobody was injured, but some damage was done to a number garden sheds and outhouses, and the windows of several nearby houses were blown out. The occupants of the house and garden where the bomb had fallen were sitting in their front room when the explosion occurred. Almost immediately afterwards, several pieces of shrapnel passed clear through the kitchen door and embedded themselves in the

Above: *Red Cross volunteers practising their skills at Old Heath School during the First World War.*

Left: *Soldiers marching along what is now Osborne Street during the First World War.*

walls of the sitting room. The couple's little daughter was found calmly sleeping in her upstairs bedroom, with no injuries whatso-ever, despite the fact that the ceiling in the room had been badly damaged. The only real casualty of the occasion was the young child's pram, which was later found in one of the outhouses in a mutilated condition.

At the time of the explosion almost everyone in the town was somewhat startled and confused, but there was very little in the way of panic. There were no blackout precautions in operation at the time and the trams continued on with their journeys regardless. In fact, it took some time for most people to realise what had actually happened. Although everyone in the town had heard the terrific explosion, many were unsure as to its cause. Some thought that there had been an accident at the Electric Light Works, while others were of the opinion that a motor car had exploded. And although the barracks was immediately plunged into darkness, the town itself remained illuminated for sometime afterwards.

In the days that followed the local and national press carried such headlines as 'East Anglia and the Baby Killers', and 'Why Cannot the Baby Killers Go Somewhere Else'. The reports also carried sev-eral photographs of the damage in Butt Road, including one of the baby whose pram had been destroyed. This was subsequently seen by Lady Colebrooke (wife of Lord Colebrooke, captain of the King's Gentlemen-at-Arms) who rang the *Daily Mail* to say that she would like to present the baby with a new pram if the father would not mind.

Soldiers inspecting bomb damage in Butt Road during the First World War.

As the war progressed, Zeppelins were seen passing over the town. Most of them drifted harmlessly by en route to London where they proceeded to drop their bombs on the capital. During once such raid, however, on the night of 24 September 1916, the L33 (the largest German airship built at the time) was damaged by anti-aircraft fire over London and was forced to make a crash landing. As the stricken airship turned towards the east coast in a attempt to escape home across the North Sea, it began to lose height fast over the Essex countryside and managed to turn towards the direction of Mersea where it found a soft landing site near Little Wigborough church.

After touching down and evacuating his crew (there was just one fatality), the German captain, Alois Bocker, set fire to the ship rather than risk it falling into British military hands, before marching his crew off in the direction of Colchester. They were met by Special Constable Edgar Nichols, who accepted their surrender and marched them off to Peldon post office. From there they were taken over to Mersea Island where they were handed over to the military.

In the weeks that followed thousands of sightseers travelled from miles around to view the burnt-out skeleton of the airship. They were charged 2d a head to view the wreckage, with the money collected being donated to the Red Cross and other war charities. For the most part those visiting the site arrived on their bicycles, while others either walked or travelled in horse-drawn carts and wagons. Among those from the Colchester area attending was fourteen-year-old Jack Ashton, who rode over on his bicycle to see the wreckage:

> When the Zeppelin came down at Wigborough I went over to see it on my bike, and I had never seen so many bikes in my life – there were fields of them. They just left their bikes lying around and went over to look at the site. There were soldiers guarding it and offering pieces of the Zeppelin frame for a tanner [6d] or something. We got several pieces of it but I don't know what happened to them – it was just a craze at the time.

Les Crick (born 1906) also remembered the event: 'I remember my father hiring a wagonette and my father and mother, aunt and uncle and cousin and I rode over to Wigborough to see it. It was quite large and was lying across these two fields, and there were crowds of people there milling around.' Les's wife Lilian (née Oakley, born 1908) could also remember the occasion: 'Although I never went to

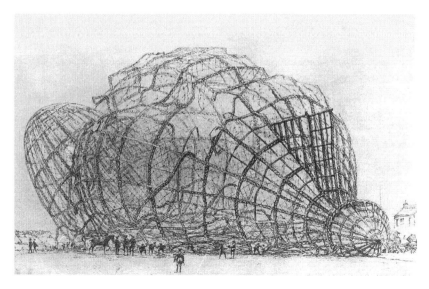

A sketch from memory of the L33 Zeppelin which crashed at Little Wigborough in 1916.

see the Zeppelin myself, I do have a brooch which was made out of a piece of the wreckage. It was cut out in the shape of the Zeppelin and put on a penny ticpin by my older brother who worked at Mumfords – I still have it about somewhere.'

When the Armistice was signed in 1918, there were celebrations in the streets of Colchester. Sidney Murrells (born 1892) recalled that people were dancing and shouting all over the place: 'They were walking up and down the High Street singing and dancing. They were putting fireworks and balloons up against the lamp-posts and the police never took any notice.' The occasion was also recalled by Alice Twyman (born 1906), who remembered walking through the town with her mother as the celebrations were taking place: 'I can remember being taken by my mother up to the hospital carrying a big Union Jack and a basket of apples. The streets were crowded with people milling around and I remember feeling a little fright ened.' And so came to an end one of the most turbulent times in our nation's history – but the peace was to be relatively short-lived.

Twenty-one years later the Second World War broke out. Blackouts, air raids and food rationing were to become the norm, and even those not actively engaged in the armed services had to do their bit to help out on the home front. For some this would have meant working round-the-clock shifts in the munitions factories, or in some other war-related activity, while for others it may have meant joining the Home Guard or taking part in regular fire-watching duties. Whatever the activity, it would have resulted in endless nights of interrupted sleep as they struggled to combine their regular day-time activities with night-time volunteer work.

URGENT.

Temporary Transfer of Population

The Government and Local Authority are extremely concerned that in response to the warning given on behalf of the Minister of Home Security by the Regional Commissioner (Sir Will Spens) comparatively so few people have taken advantage of the arrangements made for the transfer by special trains of certain classes of the Civil population of the **BOROUGH** and in particular that so many school children are still left in the town.

If invasion takes place on the Essex coast there is a very grave risk that **THIS TOWN** will be heavily bombed.

It is hoped that even if invasion is coming there may still be time to get more away, before such a situation may develop which will prevent the possibility of carrying out any further voluntary transfer of the population.

The Services will defend every inch of our land. There is no intention to retire on any portion of our coasts.

The public throughout the Country has been asked to " stay put " but special considerations apply to **THIS TOWN** which make it necessary for its population to be reduced so that it will be easier for the Army to operate. This applies particularly to children and if you have been unable to take your children away because Mother cannot go, you are earnestly urged to allow them to join a school party and go away in the care of their teachers. Others not engaged in essential work, particularly Mothers and young children, can still go with the parties and are urged to do so but a special effort is now being made to get away school children with their teachers.

Letters are coming in from the officers who took the special trains to the receiving areas, and from parents, telling of the very cordial reception our townspeople have received there. It must be realised, that, in operations on this scale, conditions for the first few hours in the reception area may be a little difficult, but every effort will be made to get all settled in suitable billets at the very earliest possible moment.

The same receiving areas will be used so that you can join your friends who have gone.

HOW TO REGISTER.

Apply at your nearest school for further particulars to-night Monday, 16th September, or to-morrow Tuesday morning.

15th September, 1940.

E. N. Mason & Sons Limited, Colchester and London.

A notice issued in September 1940 encouraging more people to leave the town before the expected invasion.

As far as the people of Colchester were concerned, the war with Germany had started days before they heard Neville Chamberlain's solemn radio announcement (11.15 a.m., Sunday 3 September 1939) that England was now at war with Germany. For on the previous Friday evening trainloads of London schoolchildren had begun arriving at St Botolph's railway station as part of a massive preplanned evacuation scheme. Alice Twyman (born 1906), a school teacher, recalled that on the very day war was declared, she was walking the streets of Colchester arranging billets for the evacuees:

> I remember that on the day war broke out – in the afternoon – my mother and I were billeting evacuees from Leytonstone. The pregnant women with children came to Lexden School, and while my mother stayed at the school helping to look after them, I worked my way along Lexden Straight Road, billeting the mothers and children. And just as I got to the end of the road, near to the Leather Bottle public house, somebody came up to me and said 'Your mother has agreed to take a mother and her six children tonight at your house, because nobody else will take them.' And I can remember racking my brains to think how many blankets and beds we could possibly make up in the house.

Following the fall of France in June 1940, the threat of invasion of Britain intensified and by September it had been decided to implement a scheme of voluntary evacuation of the young, elderly and infirm. It had been thought that if an invasion were to take place along the Essex coast then Colchester, being a military town, was likely to be heavily bombed with a high risk of civilian casualties. And so with just a few days' notice on the 11, 12 and 13 September, some 10,000 local schoolchildren, along with large numbers of parents and other relatives, left Colchester in ten specially prepared trains for the midland towns of Kettering, Stoke-on-Trent, Burton-on-Trent and Wellingborough. And so, in the space of just twelve months, Colchester had moved from being a reception area for evacuees to an evacuation area itself.

The children were accompanied by a number of local teachers who themselves had no idea of where they were going until the very last moment, such was the secrecy surrounding the whole operation. In fact, the event was so 'hush hush' that even those in the waiting reception areas were taken somewhat by surprise and were totally unprepared for the arrival and billeting of such a large number of evacuees. Joan Dobson (born 1916) was a young teacher at East Ward School when the order came through that the children were to be evacuated:

> It was decided that the children, and as many people as possible, should be evacuated there and then. It was thought that if Hitler was going to invade it would be then – the tides were right, the moon was right and there was known to be a lot of activity going on at the

other side of the Channel. So a few days later, myself and three other teachers were taken by bus with, I would think, about ninety unaccompanied children and quite a lot of parents with children to North Station and put on a train which eventually delivered us to Stoke-on-Trent. When we arrived nobody was expecting us; it was late at night and we were taken to a church hall and given something to eat, before settling down for the night on the floor of the hall. The next day, the people of Stoke-on-Trent had got to hear about this sudden evacuation from Colchester, but they weren't prepared for it. They hadn't done any billeting questionnaires or anything, so it was rather like a cattle market with people swarming into the hall and saying 'I'll have that one' and so on until all the children had been placed.

Among the thousands of local children who took part in the exercise was ten-year-old Derek Blowers (born 1930) who was evacuated to Kettering with his younger brother Michael:

We thought that being evacuated was a big adventure, to be honest. The fact that we didn't know where we were going made it even more exciting. The train left about four o'clock and the first stop was Cambridge where we were allowed a little time to stretch out legs and use the toilet. We then continued with numerable unscheduled stops through the night, eventually arriving at Kettering about midnight, and were then bedded down in a school in Beatrice Road. In the morning we were assembled into small groups and taken round the streets of Kettering by a billeting officer, knocking on various doors and asking the householder if they would take in one or two evacuees. As far as I'm aware, nothing had been pre-arranged, we just turned up at someone's door. My brother and I were eventually taken in by a middle-aged couple who had no children of their own.

Thankfully, the expected invasion failed to materialise and by Christmas most of the evacuees had decided to return home. With the immediate threat of an invasion out of the way, the town was deemed to be as safe a place as any outside the major cities. That said, however, the town was to receive its fair share of bombing throughout the war, resulting in both human casualties and the destruction of buildings. It is difficult to decide which of the numerous enemy bombing raids was the most devastating, but in terms of human lives lost, the attacks on Severalls Mental Hospital (thirty-eight lives lost) and Old Heath Laundry/Scarletts Road (five lives lost) were particularly upsetting.

36 Wordsworth Rd
Kettering
18-9-40

My Dear Mummie,
Michael and I are at Kettering staying with Mr and
Mrs Coles. We spent the
night at the school
we slept on camp beds.
We had five Blankets
between us. I shall be
writing later on. I must
close now, as Mr and Mrs
Coles our waiting to
take us out.
Love to Mummie and
Daddy from
Michael and Derek

Left: *A letter written home by Derek Blowers, a young evacuee.*

Below: *Derek Blowers today at the age of seventy-three.*

The attack on Severalls Hospital took place in the early hours of Tuesday 11 August 1942, when a single German plane dropped four 500lb bombs on the hospital. Three of the bombs scored a direct hit, killing thirty-eight patients, and injuring twenty-three others and two members of staff. In the morning, an announcement from Berlin stated that the attack was directed against military objectives. Perhaps they were aware that troops had been billeted in the hospital during the First World War and believed that the building was again being used for military purposes. Winifred Fairhead (born 1898) lived in a house within the hospital grounds and saw the attack take place: 'I can remember the night of the raid – they came over and dropped their bombs on the hospital and completely wiped out one ward, killing everybody in it. I was looking out of my

The bombing of Severalls Hospital in August 1942.

bedroom window and saw the actual plane which dropped the bombs – it came right over our house and I remember thinking whether he had just one more bomb to drop.'

The attack on Old Heath Laundry happened earlier in the war on Thursday 3 October 1940, when most of the employees were out taking their midday break. Again it was the work of a lone raider who suddenly swooped from the clouds and dropped some bombs and incendiaries in the Old Heath Road area. In the laundry a number of girls were having their lunch break when the room in which they were sitting took a direct hit. Three of the girls were killed and much of the building destroyed. One of the workers at the laundry who saw the attack was Fred Johnson (born 1902) who luckily happened to be standing a few yards away from the building when the bombs dropped: 'I heard the plane come over and got behind a tree as the bomb hit the building. Three of the girls who worked there were killed. It was terrible, they'd been sitting on the seat where they'd been having their dinner. They were killed outright. They looked like bundles of rags that had been burnt and scorched right through. If it had happened just five minutes later we'd have all been back at work and killed. It ruined the place and all the girls were terrified.'

Space does not permit any further accounts of the bombing of the town, but suffice to say the lives of those who had to endure

those troublesome times must have been clouded with fear and uncertainty as they lived in hope that they too would not fall victim to such indiscriminate killing.

Mention must also be made regarding the enormous amount of time and energy given by the huge army of volunteer workers, both men and women, from all walks of life, who toiled away in their spare time helping to maintain safety and order on the home front. Virtually everybody who was fit and able was obliged to do their bit, whether it involved helping out with local fire-watching duties, working with the air-raid wardens or perhaps becoming a member of the Home Guard. Whatever kind of work was involved it would normally have had to be done in the evenings, or perhaps overnight, before having to snatch a quick breakfast and setting off to complete a full day's work.

We are fortunate that in addition to the official record of such wartime activities, we are able to tap into the minds and memories of countless people who were privileged to play their part in the event and survive to speak for themselves. One example is that of Len Munson (born 1906) who in addition to working a full day on the land, spent several evenings a week engaged in various home defence duties: 'I had to do my share of fire-watching. One night a week I would report to my post, which was in Wyre Street, and that's where I'd stop until the siren went. Then I'd put my helmet on and

Civil Defence Volunteers practise their first aid and fire prevention skills in the playground at Old Heath School.

parade up and down the street so that if anything was to fall I'd be in a position to put it out. We had to stay on duty until six in the morning, after which time the Army would take charge of things. When I got home I'd just have time to have some breakfast before going off to work – we just had to carry on.' In addition to completing his fire-watching duties, Len was a member of the Home Guard and used to spend many a night up on the Abbey Field as part of a two-man team manning one of the many anti-aircraft rocket launchers.

Another member of the Home Guard was Dick Thorogood (born 1911) who joined one of the infantry platoons:

Members of the Home Guard in front of one their rocket launchers on the Abbey Field.

> I was working at Paxmans during the day and then did drill in the evenings. At first, we only had broomsticks and an armband. Later we got rifles and grenades, then more weaponry of other kinds. We had to be on duty all night and then go to work the next day. When they asked for volunteers for the rocket battery on the Abbey Field, I left the infantry and went for that. There were four or five lines of rocket launchers, each loaded with two rockets a piece about 5ft long. There was two members in each crew. One man had a headset on connected to the command post and would receive instructions as to co-ordinates, range and elevations etc., while the other man would set the fuses and switches. [The rockets were all fired simultaneously by an electrical circuit.] I remember on one occasion we

were all standing to, all the rockets were loaded and ready to fire, when a sergeant went into the command post to tell the operators to get a move on as we were ready to fire. What he didn't know was that the tannoy system had been left switched on and, because the reception outside wasn't too good, when the crews heard the word 'fire' they did just that and the whole battery fired its rockets, which was pretty terrifying. And unfortunately the plane was one of ours and there was a hell of a row about that – although, thankfully the plane was not shot down.

The Contemporary Town

Although life seemed to return to normal after the end of the war, there were changes afoot. A rise in the population of the town resulted in a number of major building programmes which extended into the 1950s. At the start of the war the population had been 51,000 but by 1950 it had risen to 60,000 and was still rising fast.

The town was also changing in other ways. Slowly but surely Colchester was losing its cosy market town image and developing into a modern regional centre. With hindsight it is clear that the 1960s were one of the main turning points. The electrification of the main line railway between London and Colchester, the building of the University of Essex and the opening of the town's first modern department store (Williams & Griffins), complete with multistorey car parks were surely good indicators of change.

The changes to the town's image began to accelerate even faster in the following decade. With the opening of the new Lion Walk Shopping Centre in 1975 the people of Colchester were introduced to a new concept in local shopping practice. There were further changes to the town's physical appearance. For the first time in perhaps a thousand years Culver Street was effectively cut in two, leaving this ancient back lane to the High Street as a disjointed thoroughfare. The new shopping centre must also have sent out a warning to the existing traders in the High Street, as more and more shoppers began to forsake the traditional High Street stores for the convenience of the more modern shops in the precinct.

The 1970s also saw the creation of the new Mercury Theatre, which has done much to promote the arts in the town and which is now rightly regarded as being a major asset to the town. The opening of the new purpose-built leisure centre in Cowdray Avenue, complete with swimming pool, sports pitches and concert hall facilities, added further to the transformation. The 1970s also produced a

band of sporting heroes in the form of Colchester United Football Club, who demolished the great Leeds United in the fifth round of the FA Cup in February 1971. At the time Leeds were top of the Football League and favourites to win the Cup. This was one of those occasions when most people could later recall exactly what they were doing, or where they were, at the time. In those days, of course, Leeds United were undoubtedly one of the best teams in Europe, and standing on the terraces, 2-0 up after twenty-five minutes, and hearing the crowd chanting 'Easy, Easy, Easy' is something not readily forgotten.

Another new shopping development built in Culver Street West in the late 1980s completed the transformation of the town's retail outlets, and by now the town could rightly boast some of the best shopping facilities in the region. Also, by this time, the population of the newly extended borough (1974) had risen to more than 140,000. Of course, the progress achieved in some areas has been accompanied by decline in others. There have been a number of

A 1950s view of the High Street by the local artist Charles Debenham.

Opposite: *The High Street looking west in 2003.*

casualties, particular in the field of local industry, with one of the saddest examples being the demise of the ancient Port of Colchester. For over 800 years the harbour area served the needs of the local community and as late as the 1980s was still a busy place and regarded as the second largest grain port in the country. Throughout the 1990s, however, the port entered into a spiral of downward decline and by 2001 had closed for good to commercial shipping. On a positive note, however, and notwithstanding the problems associated with the loss of the port, the entire area has recently been earmarked for regeneration with some of this work having already begun. Over 1,500 new homes are planned for the area, along with a marine centre with a tidal barrier to maintain a high water level, and a range of river-based leisure facilities. This is expected to generate up to 2,500 new jobs, helping to offset the problems caused by the decline of traditional local industries.

The overall result of this period of change and growth has, I believe, been a pleasant one. Despite the tremendous amount of new building work undertaken in the town centre and elsewhere, there remains an interesting mix of old and new with plenty of attractions for both resident and visitor alike. And this is one of the reasons why the town, which was once the capital of Roman Britain, is now regarded as the cultural capital of Essex. With attractions like the magnificent Castle Museum, which attracts more than 100,000 visitors annually, and the Grade II listed Victorian Castle Park set in 23 acres of beautifully landscaped gardens, it is easy to see why the town is high on the list of places to visit.

And, of course, it will not stop here. The town will continue to grow and prosper in the twenty-first century. Advancement based on achieving the best possible quality is now the order of the day for most council-led initiatives, which range from tourism and leisure to local housing and the environment. Already since 2001 the town has received a number of awards for its work in various fields, including the recent accolade bestowed upon the newly refurbished Hollytrees Museum, which has made it into the national top twenty of family-orientated museums – despite some very stiff competition.

And here we will end our excursion through more than 2,000 years of Colchester's history, whilst hoping that the future will prove just as interesting.

Walking Tour

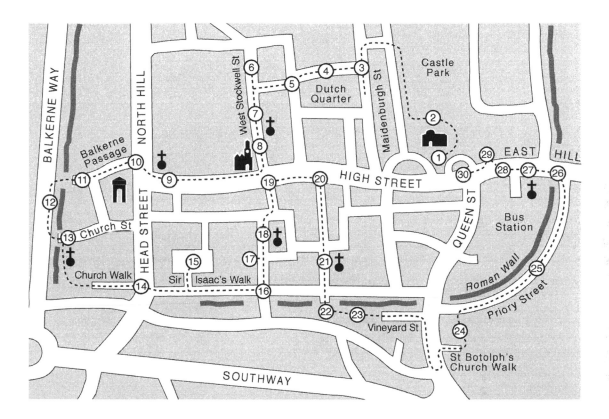

The walk starts and finishes at the War Memorial, in front of the main gates to the Castle Park, and will follow a mainly circular route of the historic town centre. The tour will include all the main historic sites of the town and should take about two hours to complete, although not necessarily all in one go. It is all fairly easy walking, with just a few small steps to negotiate around the route, although these can be avoided if necessary.

Map of the town centre showing the route of the walk. The circled numbers correspond to the directions given in the tour.

> **1 Start your tour by walking through the gates of the Castle Park and stand in front of the castle.**

Colchester Castle is the largest Norman castle keep in Europe and was built from about 1076 for William the Conqueror. The castle stands on top of the foundation podium of the great Roman Temple of Claudius which was erected here following the

Colchester Castle seen from Cowdray Crescent.

Emperor's death in AD 54 (guided tours of the vaults of the Roman temple are available inside the castle). For the most part the castle was built by using brick and stone recycled from the old Roman town. The stone is mainly septaria – a kind of fossilised mud – originally quarried by the Romans from the Essex and Suffolk coastal regions. The large windows seen in the front wall and the dome over the left side tower were added during renovation work in the eighteenth century. The small sycamore tree standing next to the dome is believed to have been planted to celebrate Wellington's victory at Waterloo in 1815. Although no documentary evidence has been found to support the claim, there does exist an early drawing of the castle dated 1817 which does indeed show a small tree in this very position – so the story could just be true. From the beginning, the castle was a royal fortress and, apart from a few short periods when it was granted to various individuals, it remained with the Crown until the reign of Charles I. In 1683, the by now redundant building was purchased by a local ironmonger, John Wheely, for the princely sum of £110, who later proceeded to demolish part of the upper floors. Precisely how much he removed is uncertain, leaving us unsure of the full height of the original castle. The foundations seen below the footbridge at the front of the building are the remains of what was once an elaborate defensive cover, or barbican, surrounding the vulnerable ground-floor doorway. The foundations on the right belong to a former Saxon chapel which was apparently rebuilt by the Normans. Curiously, the eastern end of the chapel differs by a few degrees in alignment from that of the chapel in the castle itself.

The main ground floor entrance door of Colchester Castle and the sycamore tree on top of the south-west tower.

Walking Tour

This view of the castle dating from 1817 is the earliest view showing the sycamore tree on top of the tower.

> **2 Now make your way round to the back of the castle by following the right-hand footpath. As you proceed along the eastern wall of the castle, look out for the long row of recycled Roman hypocaust (under-floor heating) bricks standing on end about halfway up the wall. And just a metre or so above these bricks, see if you can make out the line of the original first-floor temporary battlements, added during the building process in response to a supposed threat of a Danish invasion.**

The stone obelisk at the rear of the castle marks the spot where the Royalist officers, Sir Charles Lucas and Sir George Lisle, were executed following their surrender at the Siege of Colchester in 1648. When the diarist John Eveyln visited this site a few years after the siege, the place of their execution was totally devoid of grass, while the surrounding area was abounding with vegetation. The historian Philip Morant, in his *History of Colchester* (1748), makes note of a legend that had apparently become established that no grass would grow on the spot where these valiant soldiers fell. But this was probably more to do with the large numbers of people visiting the site and trampling the grass underfoot. Walking up the slope beyond the obelisk will lead you to the top of the old Norman castle ramparts and provide you an excellent view of the attractive flower borders which have been planted in the former Norman ditch.

Stone obelisk erected in memory of the Royalist officers Sir Charles Lucas and Sir George Lisle, who were executed here in 1648.

Drawing of the east wall of the castle by K. Scarff, showing the line of Roman hypocaust bricks and position of temporary battlements on the first floor.

3 Follow the footpath in the direction of the small eighteenth-century garden house in the form of a Doric temple until you reach the bottom of the rampart. Leave Castle Park via the small Ryegate Road exit and walk through into Maidenburgh Street.

You are now standing in what is known as the Dutch Quarter, so named after the Flemish weavers who settled in this area during the reign of Elizabeth I. The stone building on the corner in front of you is St Helen's chapel, which was first recorded in 1097. According to local legend the building was founded by the Empress Helena herself in the third century. The legend also states that Helena was the daughter of the legendary King Coel of nursery rhyme fame, and that her son, Constantine the Great, was born in Colchester. Of course, this is not entirely true, but whatever the truth of the matter, the building certainly stands on foundations that date from the Roman period. Like most large Roman towns, Colchester had a theatre; in fact it had two, and one of them stood right in front of you. It was built in true Roman style and would have been capable of seating about 3,500 people (compare this with our modern Mercury Theatre which has a seating capacity of just under 500). If you look carefully at the bricks lining the surface of the street leading up towards the High Street, you will see that there are some black coloured bricks lying between the red ones. The black bricks have been laid directly over the surviving foundations of the Roman theatre. If you now follow the line of black bricks up

Castle Park and houses in the nearby Dutch Quarter.

the hill you see where the curve of the former auditorium passes through the row of buildings on the right (see diagram on wall). Looking through the window of the 'Roman Theatre' you will be able to see the foundations of the building, which are just a few inches below the modern street level. Also on the wall to the right can be seen a large mural painting of what the theatre would once have looked like.

> **4 Retrace your steps to St Helen's chapel and turn left into St Helen's Lane.**

The large open space on your left as you walk along St Helen's Lane is a former Quaker burial ground, a reminder of the town's strong nonconformist background. Next on the left stands a gabled red-brick building which until 1937 was the Bluecoat school. This began as an Anglican charity school in the early eighteenth century. Colchester also had a Greencoat charity school in Priory Street which was run by the Congregationalists.

> **5 At the end of St Helen's Lane, turn left into East Stockwell Street and stand near the entrance to Quaker's Alley on the right.**

The small red-brick building on the corner of Quaker's Alley is the last surviving nineteenth-century parish schoolroom standing in the

The former Bluecoat School building, erected in 1861.

St Helen's chapel and Maidenburgh Street, showing the position of the Roman theatre wall in the street paving.

St Helen's Lane and part of the old Quaker burial ground on the left.

town centre. It was built about 1830 and stands just inside St Martin's churchyard. By the 1890s the school was bursting at the seams with more than ninety children being taught in this one room. The school finally closed when the new Stockwell Street Board School opened at the bottom of the hill in 1898. In recent years the building has been converted into a domestic dwelling with a small piece of the churchyard made available as a garden.

6 Walk along Quaker's Alley into West Stockwell Street and cross over to the far side of the road. Walk down the hill a few yards and then with your back to the large red-brick Georgian fronted building on your left, look back across the road to numbers 11 and 12 West Stockwell Street.

Opposite: *The former St Martin's parish schoolroom, built around 1830.*

As you will see from the plaque on the wall, between 1796 and 1811 this was the home of Jane and Ann Taylor. The sisters became famous for writing children's verse and rhyme, the most famous being *Twinkle Twinkle Little Star*, which was written by Jane in 1806. Jane recalled her little attic room: 'I used to roam and revel 'mid the stars, When in my attic with untold delight, I watched the changing splendours of the night.' Looking up at the little attic windows today, one can easily imagine the young girl sitting quietly looking out towards the western sky, the sun setting, the stars beginning to twinkle in the evening sky as she began to pen those enduring words.

7 Now walk a short distance back up the hill and stop opposite St Martin's church.

The oldest part of the church is the tower, which dates from the Norman period, although most of the fabric is medieval. Today the tower stands no higher than the nave, a result of damage caused by cannon fire during the Siege of Colchester. Note also the profusion of recycled Roman bricks in the tower structure, a common feature in a county almost devoid of naturally outcropping stone. If the churchyard is open see if you can find the tombstone of Jacob Ringer, a Flemish baymaker who departed this life in 1680. We know that Jacob was living in the town during the three-month siege and was later made to contribute £10 towards the hefty fine of

Above: *A timber-framed building dating from the fourteenth century in East Stockwell Street.*

11 and 12 West Stockwell Street, the former home of the children's author Jane Taylor, who wrote the poem Twinkle Twinkle Little Star *here in 1806.*

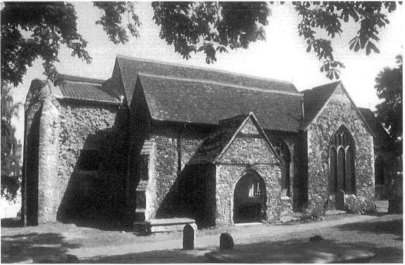

St Martin's church with its siege-damaged tower.

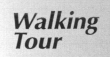

£12,000 levied on the town by Thomas Fairfax, the Parliamentarian general.

Now with your back to the church look at the Georgian building known as St Martin's House. You will notice that the building lacks the typical Georgian symmetry. See if you can spot where the left-hand section was added in the early twentieth century.

> **8 Continue up the hill and stop near the small graveyard on the corner of St Runwald Street.**

With your back to the small graveyard, look at the late fifteenth-century timber-framed building with a jettied upper storey, opposite. This is a reminder of the type of building that would have predominated in this area a few centuries ago. Turning to the graveyard, you will notice that there is no church! St Runwald's church used to stand in the middle of the High Street until its demolition in 1878.

This is also a good spot from which to view the remaining buildings on this side of the street, including the former public library (currently used as a restaurant for council employees), which opened in 1894, and the impressive tower of the Town Hall. This magnificent building is the third municipal edifice to occupy this site over the last 1,000 years. The first was Norman in origin and

Above: *The top of the Town Hall clock tower showing the statue of St Helena.*

Left: *The impressive façade of the Town Hall.*

lasted until 1843. Its Victorian replacement lasted a little over fifty years until the present structure was erected at the beginning of the last century. The building was designed by John Belcher and opened in May 1902. Building costs amounted to £55,000, which included all the interior and exterior fitments. The clock tower rises 162ft above pavement level and is surmounted with a statue representing St Helena, who is the town's patron saint. She is holding a cross in her right hand and is facing towards Jerusalem. At a slightly lower level, set at each corner, are four bronze ravens which the represent the port of Colchester. The outside of the building is also decorated with a series of marble statues depicting historical figures from the town's past. These include Boudica, the Celtic queen who led the British rebellion against Rome in AD 60, Eudo Dapifer, steward to William the Conqueror and early custodian of the castle, and the renowned scientist Dr William Gilberd who was born in the town around 1540.

> **9 Now turn right into the High Street and proceed as far as the large colonnaded building at the far end of the street. As you walk, note some of the fine architectural detail on the buildings on the opposite side of the road, particularly above the shop fronts.**

This impressive building is known locally as the Fire Office and was built in 1820. It was designed as a dual-purpose building – the upper

Shops in the High Street with impressive Victorian façades.

floor housed the Essex and Suffolk Fire Insurance Society, and the lower floor the Corn Exchange. You may be surprised to learn that most of the building, including the Doric fluted columns, is made of cast iron. The last thing that a fire insurance society wanted was for their own building to burn down!

Look also at the building to the right of the Fire Office which is currently the Co-op Bank. This was opened in 1845 as a new corn exchange to replace the building next door. Before becoming a bank it housed the town's repertory theatre.

10 Cross the road at the top of North Hill and stop at the entrance to Balkerne Passage. Glance back across the road at St Peter's church, which is the town's only church mentioned by name in the Domesday Book. It is also one of only two of the town's eight medieval churches still being used for religious services. Now walk along Balkerne Passage until you reach the large red-brick water tower.

The cast-iron-clad Essex and Suffolk Fire Office building, erected in 1820.

St Peter's church.

The water tower was built in 1882 and is known locally as Jumbo. The name derives from a famous elephant of the day at London Zoo which was sold, amidst considerable public outcry, to Barnum and Bailey's travelling circus in America. The elephant's personal keeper, Matthew Scott, was sold with him and he went on to thrill American audiences for several years until he was killed by a train in Canada. The name Jumbo was coined by the Revd John Irvine, who lived on the site of the present Mercury Theatre. Presumably not being too happy about the giant structure being erected at the bottom of his garden, he described what he considered to be a large monstrous looking building as a 'Jumbo', and the name stuck. The builders who were working on the tower eventually went to the trouble of having an elephant crafted in brass and fixed to the weather vane as a permanent reminder to the unhappy clergyman.

Opposite: *The remains of
the Roman Balkerne
gateway and the south
pedestrian footway.*

138

11 Now walk the short distance to the Balkerne Gateway, passing the Mercury Theatre on your left. The theatre has a seating capacity of 499 and was opened in 1972. It was named after the Roman messenger god, and in the Castle Museum is a particularly fine bronze statue of Mercury which was discovered in a Colchester field in the 1940s. The statue of Mercury adorning the theatre is a copy of a Renaissance figure housed in a museum in Florence.

Walking Tour

You are now looking at the oldest surviving Roman gateway in Britain which is still in use. In Roman times the gateway extended across the entire area now covered by the Hole in the Wall public house and comprised two large carriageways in the centre with a pedestrian footway on either side. Adjoining these smaller footways were D-shaped bastions which served as guardrooms for the Roman sentries. Before walking through the pedestrian footway, step down into the former guardroom on the left and take a close look at the original facing brickwork.

'Jumbo', the Victorian water tower.

12 Next walk through the gateway and turning to your left continue for a few paces before stopping in front of the Roman wall.

Above: The weather vane on the water tower showing Jumbo the elephant.

This is the best preserved section of the wall which originally encircled the town for a distance of about a mile and a half. The wall is about 8ft thick and still stands almost to its former height. It was built almost entirely from fragments of Roman brick and septaria stone, although neatly arranged courses were only used on the inner and outer surfaces. The core of the wall was filled with rubble and hardcore.

> **13 Continue along the wall to the set of steps which will take you up into Church Street. Position yourself to obtain a good view of the church tower.**

St Mary's at the Walls church is of medieval origin and was one of many buildings damaged during the Siege of Colchester in 1648. Both the church and graveyard were used as a fort by the Royalist

Walking Tour

St Mary's at the Walls church with its siege-damaged tower.

defenders, who at one stage managed to raise a small cannon to the top of the tower. This was eventually targeted by the besieging Parliamentarians, resulting in severe damage to the church and tower, and the demise of the marksman and his cannon. The church was rebuilt in the early eighteenth century, although the present nave and chancel is Victorian. The church is currently known as St Mary's Arts Centre and is a popular venue for a wide range of musical and stage productions.

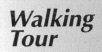

Walking Tour

14 Now walk through the churchyard and down Church Walk to arrive at Headgate Corner. (If the churchyard is closed, continue walking along Church Street before turning right into Head Street and then along to Headgate Corner.)

Before crossing the road, note the large building on the left corner of Sir Isaac's Walk opposite, which was the former residence of Sir Isaac Rebow, a wealthy clothier of Flemish descent. He was MP for Colchester for thirty years and on several occasions entertained William of Orange (William III of England, 1689-1702) here as he travelled to and from Holland. Also note the plaque on the wall to the right of Sir Isaac's Walk, showing the position of the former Roman Head Gate.

Detail of the Roman wall with alternating courses of brick and septaria stone.

Head Street, showing the former home of Sir Isaac Rebow.

Sir Isaac's Walk in the direction of Head Street.

15 Cross the road and walk along Sir Isaac's Walk, turning left into the Culver Shopping Precinct. Continue into the centre of the square.

Water fountain in the Culver shopping precinct.

Beneath you is a large underground service area for the surrounding shops, which covers nearly 2 acres. Before the site was developed, a large archaeological excavation took place which located the foundations of numerous buildings of the Roman legionary fortress which was established here in AD 43. Of particular interest was the uncovering of the main north–south roadway of the fortress which ran along in front of what is now Waterstone's bookshop, as well as the foundation walls of some of the large barrack blocks where the Roman soldiers were quartered. The fountain itself incorporates two interesting features associated with the town's history. In the centre is a sea holly plant from the root of which a local candied delicacy known as Eryngo was produced. Around the base of the sea holly are several oyster shells, symbolic of Colchester's long association with the oyster industry.

16 Return to Sir Isaac's Walk and continue until you reach Sheregate Steps.

Originally there was no gateway or opening through the Roman wall at this point and the present entrance is believed to have been made during the medieval period to provide easy access to and from St John's Abbey. Notice how well the building surrounding the gateway, which dates from around 1500, merges with the adjoining twentieth-century buildings. This is a good example of town planning in the traditional style.

17 Now walk up Trinity Street and turn left into the entrance of Tymperleys Clock Museum and stand on the lawn in front of the building.

Tymperleys is part of the former home of Dr William Gilberd (1540-1603), a renowned scientist and physician to Queen Elizabeth I (1558-1603). He was a contemporary of such learned men as Galileo and Kepler and wrote an extensive treatise on magnetism entitled *De magnete*. He was the first English scientist to accept the ideas of Copernicus and coined such terms as *electricity*

*Trinity Street: the Saxon
tower of Holy Trinity
church and the clock
tower of the Town Hall
are visible.*

Walking Tour

The Saxon arrow-head doorway leading through the tower of Holy Trinity church.

and *magnetic pole*. He was buried in Holy Trinity church, opposite. In the early twentieth century, Tymperleys came into the possession of a local industrialist named Bernard Mason. One of Bernard's passions was collecting clocks, and in particular clocks that had been crafted by Colchester tradesmen. He eventually managed to acquire about 200 clocks of varying designs and before his death gave the entire collection, as well as Tymperley's in which to house them, to the borough. The house has now been transformed into a clock museum where about sixty of the clocks are on permanent display.

18 Returning into Trinity Street, walk up as far as the church tower.

The High Street entrance to the Red Lion Hotel and Red Lion Yard.

On your left you will pass No.6 (built *c.*1690) which was formerly owned by Lady D'Arcy (Countess Rivers). Her music master was John Wilbye (*c.*1573–1638), one of England's finest composers of madrigals, who died here.

The tower of Holy Trinity church is the only Saxon monument still standing in Colchester. It dates from around 1000 and incorporates an interesting arrow-head doorway next to the street, built entirely of reused Roman bricks.

19 At the top of Trinity Street cross over into Pelham's Lane and walk through to the High Street.

From this side of the High Street you have a good view of the front of the Town Hall, with its series of marble statues gazing down on to the main street. Looking to your right you will see the Hippodrome night club, which was originally built as a variety theatre at the beginning of the last century. All of the main vaudeville stars of the day appeared here at one time or another including, the singer Marie Lloyd, Harry Champion, Little Tich and the up-and-coming comedian Charlie Chaplin, shortly before he emigrated to America.

20 Turn right and continue down the High Street as far as the Red Lion Hotel.

The Red Lion Hotel was built for John Howard (later Duke of Norfolk) in about 1481. By the early sixteenth century it seems to have been converted into an inn, known originally as the Whyght Lion, and was one the first of Colchester's inns to be used by the London coaches. Note the intricate carving on the timber work at the front of the building, and especially the carved figures of St George and the Dragon in the top corners of the main entrance.

21 Go through the entrance into Red Lion Yard and on through to the Lion Walk shopping precinct.

Dominating the shopping area is the tall Gothic spire of Lion Walk United Reformed church. If you look carefully you can see a join about halfway up the spire where it had to be replaced after breaking off during the Colchester Earthquake of 1884.

22 Walk to the end of the precinct past the church and go through the passageway to Vineyard Steps.

From the top of the steps look straight ahead into the distance to catch sight of the fifteenth-century gatehouse of St John's Abbey. The gatehouse is all that survives of this once great Benedictine Abbey which was founded here by Eudo Dapifer in 1095. At the time of the Dissolution of the Monasteries during the reign of Henry VIII, the abbot of St John's stubbornly refused to hand over the Abbey and its lands to the king, and was subsequently arrested for treason. Following a protracted trial in London he was returned to Colchester, where he was dragged through the streets on a sledge before being hanged.

23 Either walk down the steps or take the lift to Vineyard Street and follow the line of the Roman wall through the car park.

The remains of St Botolph's Priory. This is the view north across the nave from the former cloisters.

This section of the Roman wall has a distinct medieval feel about it with most of the buildings sitting on top of the wall. Look out for the Roman drain which would have carried waste and surface water from the street behind into the town ditch.

24 Continue to the end of Vineyard Street and turn right into St Botolph's Street. Walk down to the traffic lights, cross the road, turn left and then quick right into St Botolph's Church Walk. Walk round to the left of the church until you come to the ruins of St Botolph's Priory.

The priory was founded around 1100 and was the first house of Augustinian canons in England. All that remains today, however, is part of the original western front, with its superbly carved Norman archway, and a section of the nave. Once again, note the liberal use of Roman brick in its construction. One can also make out part of what would have been a large round window above the central archway. If you now walk through the arched doorway into the nave you will be able to see how far the original church extended by taking note of the ground markings. Unlike the Benedictine order, who kept themselves quite apart from the general public, the Augustinians allowed the public to make use of the priory church. And it was this alliance with the general public that saved the complex from total ruin at the time of the Dissolution. Following the Dissolution, the priory church became the principal place of worship in the town until its partial destruction during the Siege of Colchester.

> **25 Leave the churchyard by the Priory Street entrance and turn right, following the line of the Roman wall.**

As you walk along this section of the Roman wall you will notice that it is not in such good repair as the section near the Balkerne Gateway. There are, however, a number of medieval bastions to be seen, added in the fourteenth century. Towards the end of the street

Priory Street, showing the line of the Roman wall.

there are large areas of the wall that have been repaired with red brick. Most of this damage occurred during the siege in 1648.

26 Continue walking along Priory Street and turn left onto East Hill. Walk up the hill until you come to St James's church.

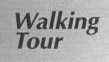

St James's church is the largest of the town's medieval churches and stands just inside the Roman wall. It dates in part from the twelfth century and originally consisted of just a narrow nave. The chancel, tower and nave aisles are all later additions. The East Gate of the town, which spanned the roadway just below the church, survived until 1674.

27 Continue walking up the hill until you come to East Hill House on the left. Note the old public drinking fountain set into the brick wall on the left.

St James's church, the largest of Colchester's medieval churches.

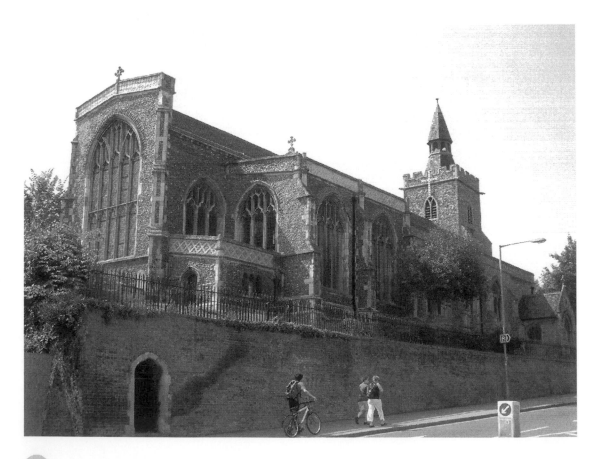

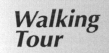

Walking Tour

The old public fountain which was erected in the brick wall alongside the pavement in 1864 by members of the Round family who lived nearby.

The Roman Doric porch of East Hill House.

This fine Georgian building was built by George Wegg between 1725 and 1750. In order to build the house and provide sufficient room for the spacious grounds, nine adjacent properties had to be demolished. George's younger brother Samuel was a very successful lawyer and businessman, rising to become the governor of the Hudson Bay Company.

If you now look over to the opposite side of the road you will have a good view of the brick-fronted Grey Friars Adult Community College. The central part of the building was erected in 1755 by the Revd John Halls of Easthorpe, and the side wings were

added in 1908. The house is named after the Franciscan (grey friars) friary which was founded here in the thirteenth century. In 1920 the building was purchased by the county council for the Colchester County High School for Girls, and in about 1970 became a centre for further education.

The Georgian façade of Grey House, erected in 1755.

28 Continue along the street to the Minories.

The Minories was the former home of the Boggis family, who were wealthy cloth merchants. The house is Tudor in origin and was first acquired by Isaac Boggis (1699–1762) in 1731, who went on to make his fortune in the bay trade. When he died in 1762 the house passed to his eldest son Thomas (1738–1790), and it was he who had the house remodelled in the Palladian style in 1776. Note the Doric porch surmounted by two tiers of brick bay windows, an unusual feature in Colchester. Note also the impressive four-gabled building opposite. This is known as the East Lodge and Gate House, and dates from around 1600. The building is of timber-frame construction and has rusticated plasterwork on the frontage.

29 At the traffic lights, cross the road and enter the gateway into the grounds of Hollytrees Museum.

The internationally renowned historian Nikolaus Pevsner described Hollytrees as 'the best eighteenth-century house in Colchester'. The house was built around 1718 by Elizabeth Cornelisen, a wealthy

High Street: East Lodge and the Gate House to the left, and Winsley's House to the right.

Hollytrees House in the early twentieth century.

widow who had purchased the site from the estate of the previous owners. Unfortunately, she died soon after the new building was completed and the house passed to her niece, Sara Webster, the daughter of a wealthy West India merchant, who was married to Ralph Creffield. The couple decided to occupy the house, which became known as Creffields. Within a short period of time, however, Ralph died and Sara went on to marry Charles Gray in about 1726. Charles Gray was a local lawyer and respected antiquarian, and he wasted no time before modifying his house and gardens. One of his first tasks was to plant the now famous holly trees at the front of the house. This act is noted in his diary where he writes: '1729 – The hollys planted in ye middle of March and grassed in ye kitchen garden.' Hollytrees is now a museum which concentrates mainly on Colchester's recent history.

30 Finally make your way back to the War Memorial where our tour ends.

This is the end of the tour, but before we finish the War Memorial itself deserves some comment. The monument, which incorporates bronze statues of Victory, Peace and St George, was erected in 1923. The War Memorial and its setting, including the castle and Hollytrees Museum, were all acquired for the town by Sir Weetman Pearson (Lord Cowdray), MP for Colchester from 1895 to 1910.

Opposite: The War Memorial.

Further Reading

Benham, H. *Essex at War*. Benham & Co. Ltd, 1945

Britnell, R.H. *Growth and decline in Colchester 1300-1525*. Cambridge University Press, 1986

Brown, A.F.J. *Colchester 1815-1914*. Essex County Council, 1980

Brown, A.F.J. *Colchester in the 18th Century*. Published privately, 1969

Cole, W. (ed.) *The East Anglian Earthquake*. The Essex Field Club, 1885

Cooper, J. (ed.) *Victoria County History of Essex, vol. 9: Colchester*. Oxford University Press, 1997

Cromwell, T. *History of Colchester* (2 vols). 1825

Crummy, P. *City of Victory*. Colchester Archaeological Trust, 1997

Cutts, E.L. *Historic Towns Series: Colchester*. 1888

Haining, P. *The Great English Earthquake*. Robert Hale, 1976

Hedges, J. & Denney, P. *Starvation and Surrender: Matthew Carter's Siege of Colchester*. JMH Publications, 2002

Jones, P. *The Siege of Colchester*. Tempus Publishing Ltd, 2003

Morant, P. *History and Antiquities of the Most Ancient Town of Colchester*. 1748

Phillips, A. *Ten Men and Colchester*. Essex Record Office, 1985

Sealey, P. *The Boudican Revolt against Rome*. Shire Archaeology, 1997

Index

*Page references in **bold** are to illustrations*

If you are interested in purchasing
other books published by Tempus, or in case you have
difficulty finding any Tempus books in your local bookshop,
you can also place orders directly through our website

www.tempus-publishing.com

or from

BOOKPOST
Freepost, PO Box 29,
Douglas, Isle of Man
IM99 1BQ
Tel 01624 836000
email bookshop@enterprise.net